The Rights of Man,
The Reign of Terror

Susan Banfield

The Rights of Man, The Reign of Terror:

The Story of the French Revolution

J.B. LIPPINCOTT NEW YORK

The Rights of Man, The Reign of Terror: The Story of the
French Revolution
Copyright © 1989 by Susan Banfield
Printed in the U.S.A. All rights reserved.
Typography by Andrew Rhodes
1   2   3   4   5   6   7   8   9   10
First Edition

Library of Congress Cataloging-in-Publication Data

Banfield, Susan.
   The rights of man, the reign of terror : the story of the French
Revolution / by Susan Banfield.
      p.   cm.
   Bibliography: p.
   Includes index.
   Summary: Recounts the political, social, and economic turmoil
that took place during the French Revolution.
   ISBN 0-397-32353-0 : $. — ISBN 0-397-32354-9 (lib. bdg.) : $
   1. France—History—Revolution, 1789–1799—Juvenile literature.
2. Human rights—France—History—18th century—Juvenile literature.
[1. France—History—Revolution, 1789–1799.]   I. Title.
DC148.B35 1989   89-2742
944.04—dc19   CIP
                                                                            AC

Cartography by Robert Romagnoli

CONTENTS

944.04
Ban

The Rights of Man, The Reign of Terror

CHAPTER

1

Chronology

PRIOR TO 1789

	rise of the bourgeoisie
	closing of the ranks of the nobility
	worsening of France's economic condition
1788	the revolt of the nobility

•

1789

May 5	opening of the Estates General
June 17	third estate declares itself the National Assembly
July 14	storming of the Bastille

Chapter One

THE REVOLT OF THE THIRD ESTATE

The King yawned as one of his valets threw back the heavy brocade curtains that surrounded the royal bed on four sides. The light that streamed through the tall casement windows now flooded the entire room. The King rose at once. After he had said his morning prayers, the elaborate process of dressing him began. First, one of his valets shaved him. Then, one at a time, each nobleman who had earned the privilege of waiting on the King handed him the article that was officially his to present. One might hand him his stockings, another his satin breeches, yet another his garters. Once he had been dressed, the King's hair was carefully curled and powdered.

Meantime, a similar little drama was being enacted in the bedroom of the Queen. There, at the center of a circle of softly swishing silks, stood Queen Marie Antoinette. She shivered in the chill morning air as she waited for the appointed lady-in-waiting to hand her her undergarments. Several others then helped her into her dress—one of the three new ones she had bought for that week.

The royal husband and wife would not see each other until noon Mass. They would then take the midday meal together, seated side by side at a small table. Dinner was far from an intimate meal for two, however. The women of the royal family and other noblewomen of

Louis XVI (1754–1793), King of France 1774–1793. In this portrait by the French artist Ducreux, Louis's reluctance to confront the difficult issues that faced his nation shows clearly in his face. *The Bettmann Archive.*

the court sat on stools encircling the royal table. Beyond them was a crowd of spectators eager for the chance at a glimpse of their rulers. Servants brought out one heavy silver serving dish after another. The King, conscious of the dozens of pairs of eyes that followed his every move, might help his wife to the dishes she fancied that day, but it was unlikely that there would be any further conversation between them. That would have been too informal.

Meanwhile, the sun was also rising on a crude mud cottage in Picardy. Jean Flavier and his family could not see it, as windows were a luxury way beyond their means. But the light creeping in under the door let them know it was time to be up and about. Jean's wife Marie shivered as she quickly pulled on her tattered old linen dress and wooden shoes.

She ripped off a piece of bread for herself and her youngest son. The bread was made of grain so coarsely ground that pieces of straw still stuck in the loaf. Marie wrapped another hunk of the bread for her husband to take out to the fields, sticking in a few small apples along with it.

In sullen silence Jean Flavier took the small parcel that his wife pressed into his hand. Feelings of rage and hopelessness swirled inside him. The bailiff was due to come any day to inquire about the grain they had borrowed from the lord last winter. After the Church took its due from their small garden, what was left would scarcely last them till Christmas. Surely their house would be stripped.

The sun was rising up above the trees now. Jean knew he was late again in setting out for the fields. But he could not seem to care.

Except for a difference in setting—a crowded top-floor room in a run-down old building in a suburb of Paris where artisans lived—a very similar scene was at that same time being enacted at the home of Jean Flavier's cousin Pierre. Pierre Flavier, near starvation one winter, had moved his family to Paris to find work. He, too, was up well before sunrise. He scurried around, rubbing his hands together to warm up, for the family's room was cold. As Pierre's wife wrapped her husband a small lunch to take to work, she also sighed.

Her sigh came of realizing that today was market day. That meant she would have to leave her new infant daughter with her younger sister and brave the crowds to buy bread for the family. She shuddered at the thought. Last market day the crowds had been restless, for the city had raised the price of bread yet again. She understood the anger. She shared it—it would now cost four days of her husband's wages to pay for the bread their family would eat in a week. But she also feared the anger. And rumor had it that today the price would climb higher still. Perhaps if she got there early . . .

For generations the peasants, the workers, and the kings and queens of France had been living lives much like those described above. The contrast between the existence of the monarchs and that of the common men and women was extreme, and had been so for some time. Few seemed to question it. The form of government that permitted and helped to create these contrasts, absolute monarchy, was accepted as a fact of life. An absolute monarch, such as the King of France was, had the power to raise armies, to declare war, and to make and unmake laws—and he was answerable for his actions to no one save God.

Yet, in a matter of years, all this was to change. Not only the form of government, but also the people's unquestioning acceptance of both the government and the place in life assigned them under it, would be swept away. In their place would be a whole new government and new ways of living and thinking and viewing the world. France would no longer have a king and queen. And the common people would know the taste of liberty and equality.

The French Revolution—the name given to the series of events between 1789 and 1794 that led to sweeping changes in the government and society of France—was one of the most momentous occurrences of recent times. What caused it? For nearly two centuries historians have debated that question. Like most turning points in history, the French Revolution was a complex event that had many different causes.

Characters in the Revolutionary Drama: *Louis XVI and Marie Antoinette*

All his life, Louis XVI felt unsure of himself, both as a man and as a sovereign. He stood five foot seven, a height impressive for the era. He was also enormously strong. He loved to hunt, and he could race through the woods after game for days on end. Yet, despite his strength and stature, Louis's presence was not a commanding one. He was slightly flabby, especially around the chin and mouth. He was persistently clumsy, and his manner was awkward and ungainly.

Those who knew the King closely also noted that he had a genuinely good heart. He hated to hear of the disasters or accidents that befell others. He was deeply religious, attending Mass daily. Yet few ever got to see the kindheartedness that might have endeared him to his people. The insecure King was forever presenting a mask to the public. Often it was that of the gruff, strong ruler. In their times of personal hardship, Louis could barely bring himself to offer his courtiers anything but a few unfeeling words delivered in harsh tones. Other times he reverted to outright childishness, playing pranks on his pages or roughhousing with them.

Louis XVI seemed genuinely to dislike the job he had been born to do. He made an effort to go through the motions he thought were required of him. He would spend long hours poring over various accounts. He built a vast library and spent many hours reading. Yet he avoided, in all this activity, the difficult thinking through of problems and decision making that are at the heart of ruling well. It seemed Louis was happiest when busy at the various crafts—such as wood- and metalworking and masonry—with which he often occupied himself. He was once heard to remark, upon hearing that one of his ministers had left his office, "Why can't *I* resign too?"

Louis's Queen, Marie Antoinette, was as outspoken, willful, and unreserved as her husband was stiff, shy, and self-doubting. The fifteenth child of the Empress of Austria, she had been brought to France at the age of fourteen to marry the future King. She was pretty, affectionate, and vivacious, and she seemed to adjust quickly to her new life. But it was inevitable that, in the face of such a momentous change, fears and insecurities lurked beneath this assured air—fears perhaps not that different from those of the King.

All her life, Marie Antoinette had a terrible fear of simply being still. She felt driven to fill every waking moment with bustle and distraction. In a frantic quest for personal fulfillment, she flitted from one activity to another—playing with her dogs, embroidering, playing cards, going for fast drives in her personal cab. With the royal purse at her disposal, the Queen's activities took on a larger-than-life quality. She had amateur dramatic productions staged so that she might act in them; she had a miniature country village built for her on the grounds of Versailles so that she might dress up as a dairymaid and play at being a country maiden. She spent vast sums yearly on clothes, buying a new dress nearly every other day.

The Queen indulged herself in other ways as well. She was like a spoiled child who had to have her own way. She was frequently impatient with the web of rules that governed the lives of the royal family and often simply refused to abide by them. What aroused the disapproval of her subjects even more was her habit of expressing whatever she happened to be feeling. The

Marie Antoinette (1755–1793), Queen of France 1774–1793. The Queen was known for her extravagant taste. She is shown here in one of the elaborate, plumed hairstyles that she helped to popularize. Some fashionable ladies, following Marie Antoinette's example, had coiffures so high that they had to ride with their heads sticking out of their carriage windows. *The Bettmann Archive.*

French expected their King and Queen to be models of correct behavior. Yet Marie Antoinette laughed, cried, threw fits of temper, and teased her husband—whether or not the time and place were appropriate for such behavior. She also developed a reputation as a libertine, and she seemed to take pleasure in shocking the men and women of the royal court.

Unlike the King, the young Queen was eager to have a hand in the government of the nation. She had strong opinions on how France ought to be ruled and often was successful at getting her husband to follow her lead in politics. Unfortunately, Marie Antoinette's political views were seldom the product of thoughtful, disinterested consideration of a problem. They were more often impulsive and bound up with the desire to protect her own interests.

Marie Antoinette was not a terrible queen. Nor, any more than her husband, was she a horrible person. Many of her antics were understandable in light of the difficulty of being thrust into the role of ruler of a strange nation at the tender age of fifteen.

Both Louis and his Queen were merely average monarchs. "Nature had made [Louis] an ordinary man, who would have done well in some obscure station," wrote the great revolutionary salon mistress Madame Manon Roland. She might have said the same of Marie Antoinette. Perhaps if either Louis or his Queen had been a more capable ruler, the crisis that eventually destroyed the monarchy of France might have been averted. But they were not. Louis, Madame Roland went on to say, was "lost through mediocrity in a difficult period when he could have been saved only through genius and strength."

The Three Estates

You have already seen how sharp a contrast existed between the lives of the King and Queen of France and those of peasants and Parisian laborers. In the days of the *ancien régime*, the name commonly given to the hierarchical society of prerevolutionary France, such a contrast was typical of the divisions that existed among the various groups in the population. Along with the contrasts, there was much friction among the groups.

French society traditionally had been divided into three classes, or orders, called the "three estates." These were the clergy, the nobility, and the common people (everyone else).

The First Estate: THE CLERGY

The first of the three estates, the clergy, was a group as much marked by division and inequality as was society as a whole. The upper clergy were generally noblemen by birth. On the eve of the Revolution nearly every bishop and archbishop was a nobleman. Some abbots—men who headed communities of monks—enjoyed annual incomes of several hundred thousand livres. (The livre was then the basic unit of currency in France, as the dollar is now in the United States. Its value was about $4.05 in modern dollars.)

The majority of the first estate, however, were not rich. Many curés, or parish priests, came from peasant families, and their lives differed little from those of the villagers they served. They lived on modest, fixed incomes or survived solely on the small fees they charged to perform marriages, baptisms, and burials. Country priests, dressed in threadbare habits, spent their days trudging rough country roads to tend to the problems of those in their charge.

Resentment toward the Church had grown during the 1700s, especially among members of the third estate. There were several reasons for this. First, although many individual priests, monks, and nuns were poor, the Church as an institution was enormously rich. Its members numbered only about a hundred thousand—less than 1/2 of 1 percent of the population—yet the Church owned over 10 percent of the land in France. In some towns such as Angers in the Loire valley, southwest of Paris, nearly half the land was occupied by Church buildings and grounds. Also, no member of the clergy had to pay

This contemporary cartoon shows a common view of the relationships among the three estates on the eve of the Revolution. The first estate, or clergy, and the second estate, the nobility, are pictured as being supported by a haggard, overworked third estate, the common people. The first estate is represented by a well-fed clergyman, one of that estate's many aristocratic members. *Musée Carnavalet (Art Resource/Lauros-Giraudon)*.

taxes, though the Church expected all parishioners to pay it an annual sum, called a "tithe." The tithe was officially 10 percent of the value of a family's crops and flocks. Although in practice it averaged somewhat less than 10 percent, still this especially grated on members of the third estate, who were already heavily taxed.

Still another cause of resentment toward the first estate was the great power the Church had in the affairs of the nation. The Church had its own courts of law, controlled most of the schools in France, and was involved in the censorship of much that was published. Members of the clergy frequently had great influence over government policy making. This might have been acceptable had the Church inspired the people with its reputation for upright behavior. In general, people had respect for their local parish priests. However, the actions of some monks, nuns, and members of the upper clergy helped to give the Church a reputation for corruption.

Bishops abandoned the people in their dioceses to accept invitations to live at court. There, many traded their clerical robes for the fashionable silks of the courtiers and gave themselves over to a life of worldly power and riches. Well-to-do young women might spend several years in elegant convents, only to emerge more eligible marriage prospects than ever—because of their "sacrifice." As a result of all this, distrust of and resentment toward the first estate were on the rise.

The Second Estate: THE NOBILITY

A farmer in the Loire valley was accustomed to working his own land. Throughout the growing season he and his youngest son labored under the hot sun. He was frugal with his money, careful to make his modest yearly income stretch to meet the expenses of his family and their ramshackle farmhouse. Not far off, in Nantes, another landowner enjoyed a fortune of several million livres. His sons had the best tutors and dressed in fine silks. To which orders did these two men belong?

The first was a noble, a member of the second estate, and the second a commoner, or member of the third estate. The point here is that wealth was not what made someone a member of the nobility. There were a number of impoverished nobles who were forced to help with their own farmwork and to count their pennies. On the whole, however, the French nobility *were* a very wealthy group. All together they numbered about four hundred thousand—about one and a half percent of the country's total population—yet owned one fifth of the nation's lands—twice as much as the Church. Many nobles lived in elegant châteaux and manor houses. Others, who lived at court with the King and Queen, might spend over forty thousand livres a year on dinner parties alone. A significant number of the nobles who lived in the provinces, however, lived modestly, with little to distinguish them outwardly from their nonnoble neighbors.

Rather than wealth, it was a person's ancestry, values, and way of life that were traditionally thought to define the nobility. The commonly accepted theory of the day was that the nobles were the descendants of the warriors who had helped the early Frankish kings conquer the land of France, and whose principal job was to continue to help them defend it. As a result of this ancestry and heritage, nobles were assumed to live according to values of courage, service, and refinement. Although, as mentioned above, there were exceptions; nobles were not supposed to work for a living. In fact, they were forbidden by law from engaging in trade. They were expected to live off the income derived from their lands, and thus be free for service to the King or for cultural pursuits. Indeed, the French nobility of the seventeenth and eighteenth centuries were largely responsible for a culture and manner of living that have been regarded ever since as among the most civilized the world has ever known. It was in the fashionable salons held by noblewomen that such great thinkers and writers as Voltaire, David Hume, and even Benjamin Franklin became known and their ideas became popular.

However, what most readily distinguished the nobles in the eyes of outsiders were their privileges. Most important among these were their financial privileges. Prior to 1695 nobles had been free from all tax-ation. Since that time the kings of France had levied several taxes on the nobility. Still, nobles were exempt from the main direct tax, the *taille*. And to offset what they had to pay, the nobility enjoyed the privilege of collecting various feudal dues from the peasants who worked on their land.

Nobles also enjoyed a number of other privileges. They had exclu-sive hunting rights on their land—including the right to let their hounds trample all over a vassal's crops while pursuing their prey. They had the right to trial in special courts, the right to wear a sword in public, and the right to display a coat of arms.

Finally, the nobility played a central role in the affairs of the French nation. Nearly all of the King's ministers were nobles. Most army officers were nobles. High offices in the Church nearly always went to men of noble birth. And because Louis XVI was a relatively weak king, during his reign nobles throughout the country slowly began to claim more power for themselves in governing the affairs of their regions.

Because of the great privileges nobles enjoyed, many members of the third estate were eager to acquire noble status themselves. Despite the theory that nobility was something in the blood and could not be bought, in actual fact, ever since the reign of Louis XIV, many wealthy commoners had been able to buy noble titles and positions. Over the hundred-year span from the reign of Louis XIV to that of Louis XVI, between sixty-five hundred and ten thousand men were newly en-nobled. The continual swelling of the ranks of the nobility with newly ennobled commoners created tensions, both within the nobility itself and between noblemen and the members of the third estate who had not yet been able to join its ranks.

Since the seventeenth century sharp divisions had arisen between the various groups of nobles. Those who could trace their lineage back for many generations wanted to protect the "purity" of their ranks and slow the flood of commoners into their order. Many of these nobles were poor and felt threatened by the wealthy newcomers to noble status.

By the 1780s the ranks of the nobility had become increasingly difficult to enter. In 1781 a ruling was passed that restricted careers as army officers—regarded as among the most prestigious careers possible—to men who came from at least four generations of noble stock.

The nation's thirteen regional courts, called *parlements*, also began to close their membership to nonnobles. Once, both nobles and wealthy local merchants had sat on the historic *parlements*, the highest courts in the land. But by the latter part of the eighteenth century they were almost entirely noble.

This closing of the ranks of the nobility, while far from total, bred resentment among the wealthier commoners.

The Third Estate 1: THE BOURGEOISIE

The third estate is not as easy to define as the first and second. Simply put, this order was comprised of everyone in France who was not a member of either of the other two. Such a group was bound to be diverse. Its members ranged from wealthy silk merchants and learned doctors to small shopkeepers and penniless beggars. However, the third estate can be roughly divided into several main groups. These were the bourgeoisie, the peasantry, and the urban workers.

Traditionally, "bourgeois" meant "town dweller." Yet by the 1700s this definition no longer applied. Many who lived in the nation's cities could not claim to be bourgeois. On the other hand, a number of bourgeois families lived in the countryside. What, then, was a bourgeois? The answer to that question depended principally on how a man made his living. Just as the second estate was set apart by the fact that its members were not supposed to work to earn a living, the bourgeoisie were set apart from the rest of the third estate by the fact that they did not earn a living by coarse, manual labor. The bourgeoisie was comprised of the nation's merchants, skilled artisans, lawyers, doctors, and other professionals.

Up to the eve of the Revolution, there was little distinction between the wealthy bourgeoisie and the nobility of eighteenth-century France. Since most bourgeois hoped one day to join the noble ranks, in the meantime they took noble values as their own and copied noble ways of life. As a result of these shared values and of their shared respect for noble status as the supreme goal in life, the bourgeoisie had little consciousness of itself as a class apart. Far from feeling antagonistic toward noblemen, most bourgeois simply hoped to become one of them.

However, by the second half of the eighteenth century, tension had begun to build between the two groups. As more and more lawyers found they would not be admitted to the local *parlements*, as recently ennobled bourgeois found that, despite their new titles, their bourgeois backgrounds would block them from careers in the army, resentment toward the second estate slowly began to fester. As late as 1788 it still was not strong enough to cause a rift between the two classes. But the tensions it caused would erupt soon enough.

The Third Estate 2: PEASANTS

The largest segment of the third estate was the peasantry. A peasant was a commoner who dwelt in the country. The vast majority of peasants made their living by some form of manual labor—either farming, working at such crafts as weaving, or some combination of the two. Unlike peasants in many other countries of the time, many peasants in France actually owned some land.

Still, only a minority of French peasants were able to achieve self-sufficiency. Most led rough and meager lives, were plagued by droughts and famines, and were hounded by tax collectors. Many had to supplement their farming with work as day laborers, had to migrate to the cities to find work as weavers, or had to find other sources of extra income. As the population of the country grew and manual work became relatively scarcer, thousands turned to begging and petty crime to put food in their mouths.

In the second half of the 1700s, conditions for peasants worsened dramatically. From 1770 on, France was hit by a series of poor harvests. Most of these affected several provinces, but in 1788 the harvest was poor everywhere. As a result, the price of bread, the principal food for most of the French, rose drastically. Wages, however, remained fairly stable. Since most peasants relied heavily on paid labor to supplement their farming, the bad harvests spelled crisis for many of them.

In addition to the bad harvests, the peasantry was hit hard by a steep increase in taxes from the year 1749 on. Peasants had always been the most heavily taxed group in the nation. Of all the population groups, they alone could claim no exemptions. A typical peasant paid a bewildering round of taxes, dues, and tithes. Most of these increased in the 1700s, and refusal to pay brought stiff penalties. For failure to pay the salt tax alone, thirty-four hundred people were imprisoned each year.

As they tried to reassert the power they felt they were losing to the rising bourgeoisie, local nobles became stricter about collecting the dues owed them. All this fell on the heads of the already strapped peasantry. By 1789 tensions in the French countryside had reached a new peak.

The Third Estate 3: URBAN WORKERS

The urban workers of France were a tiny minority compared with the nation's great masses of peasants. Yet their influence during the Revolution would be tremendous—out of all proportion to their numbers. For this reason they deserve separate mention.

The narrow streets and tall tenement buildings typical of the sections of Paris where the city's working people lived can be seen in this photograph taken in 1865. In the 1780s masters, journeymen, and less skilled workmen often lived in the same building. However, a family's rank in the guild hierarchy was shown by floor, with the first floor going to a master and the top reserved for the poorest tenants. Thus, their living quarters encouraged interaction between workers and masters but at the same time sharpened distinctions and resentments. *The Bettmann Archive.*

"Down with the rich! Down with the rich! Long live the third estate!" the cries went up. They were accompanied by a pelting of stones and a clatter of pikes as the mob descended on the large Reveillon wallpaper factory in the east of Paris.

One of the infamous street scenes of the Revolution? Not quite. The Reveillon riots took place in April of 1789, over two months before the storming of the Bastille. Although not actually part of the Revolution, they do much to reveal the mood of the city's working people on the eve of the great revolt.

For generations the lives of working people in France's cities had changed very little. The men who worked in Paris's textile, glass, paper, and other industries were concentrated in the eastern suburbs, areas where narrow, winding streets were lined with tall, often aging apartment buildings. The segregation between the working-class districts and those where the city's wealthier citizens dwelt was so complete that it was unusual for a worker to catch a glimpse of a noble.

Despite humble surroundings, the working life had its rewards. Most workplaces were small and congenial; in Paris, each employed an average of sixteen or seventeen artisans. Reveillon's factory had employed three hundred and fifty, but such instances were exceptions. Most workingmen belonged to guilds, which gave them certain economic privileges and the opportunity to work together with their fellows.

But in the eighteenth century the life of workers had gradually worsened. Guilds made it difficult for men to rise to the rank of master, and tensions between masters and those under them had grown. Also despite a steady rise in the prices of most goods, workers' wages did not keep pace. Working families found that it was more and more of a stretch to afford the bread that was their main staple. In times of poor harvests, it became nearly impossible.

In the years preceding the Revolution, unrest among workers rose. For the most part, the workers' instinctive response in times of hardship was to demand that the government lower the price of bread. The unrest most frequently took the form of bread riots. With economic hardship setting them on edge, the workers began more and more frequently to strike against their employers as well. Violent protests began even before the Revolution started.

While none of the mounting tensions within and between social groups of themselves caused the Revolution, they certainly made for an atmosphere that was likely to ignite, given a sufficient spark.

The Influence of the Enlightenment

Chatter filled the high-ceilinged drawing room. The light from chandeliers and candelabra danced delightfully off tall mirrors and many-paned windows. Men in powdered wigs and women in high coiffures talked gaily with one another. Conversation ran from the new craze for the color puce (a brownish purple), to theories about magnetism, to the latest gossip about a court member's mistress. Then, all of a sudden, a hush came over the crowd. Attention turned to a stately looking gentleman who had just entered the room. His dress seemed embarrassingly simple compared with that of the others, yet a circle of men and women quickly gathered around him. In no time, their earlier exchanges were replaced by animated talk about the gentleman's latest treatise on political philosophy.

Setting the Scene:
Bread for Paris

In 1789 Paris was the second largest city in Europe. Over six hundred thousand persons lived there. And for nearly every one of those six hundred thousand, bread was the mainstay of his or her diet. The average French worker ate one four-pound loaf a day. In those days before trains, tractors, and modern agriculture, the supplying of bread for such a population was a major production—and, not surprisingly, often a major problem as well.

Most of the farmland within a thirty-mile radius of Paris had been set aside expressly for growing the grain needed to make the bread for the city's residents. Yet even this was not enough. A number of large merchants became wealthy by importing grain from the provinces and, in times of failed harvests, from as far away as North Africa.

Once grain was obtained, it had to be ground into flour. There were over four thousand mills on the outskirts of Paris set up just for this purpose. In some areas hundreds of windmills dotted the countryside. All the ground flour was taken to Les Halles, the city's market, where it was purchased by bakers.

The bakers of Paris were divided into three groups. There were about two hundred who had earned the title of "city baker," which meant they had the privilege of being allowed to set up shop in central Paris. Then there were three hundred or so bakers of the faubourgs, or suburbs, whose shops were located in the outlying districts of the city. But the amount of bread these two groups could produce was limited. The slack was taken up by itinerant bakers—those who baked their bread on the outskirts of Paris and had to carry it in to market each day.

Bakers of all three groups did backbreaking work—and for scant reward. Many had customers who bought on credit and did not pay their debts. Itinerant bakers had to contend with a law that forbade them to take out at the end of the day any bread they had brought in that morning. This meant they were frequently forced to sell their wares cheaply at closing time. Bakers were often in debt.

The production and sale of bread was a major preoccupation of the Paris police. There were rules governing which bakers were allowed to make rolls and which fine wheat bread. There were rules saying which grade of bread could be sold by the loaf (only white) and which grades had to be sold by weight (the brownish-white and brown breads eaten by the common people).

There was the rule, already mentioned, forbidding itinerant bakers to leave the city with any of the bread they had brought in that morning. All of these had to be enforced. In addition, the police were responsible for monitoring the weight and quality of bread sold, a responsibility they took very seriously.

Still, despite these heroic efforts to ensure an adequate supply of bread for the people, complaints about the quantity, quality, or price of bread were chronic. Riots at bakers' shops were not uncommon, and one of the pieces of information the Lieutenant of Police awaited most eagerly each morning was a report on the status of the bread markets at Les Halles. In fact, the scarcity of bread in Paris played a significant role in the onset of the French Revolution.

Such evenings had become commonplace occurrences in Paris in the 1700s. All over the capital city, well-to-do women held these salons, at which members of society mixed with the prominent artists, writers, and thinkers of the day. The salons were part of an important movement called the Enlightenment, which changed the way many people in France thought. It is questionable how seriously most of the men and women of the salons took the new ideas to which they were exposed. Still, many new ideas did gain popularity in the 1700s and were among the causes of the Revolution that broke out in 1789.

Since the 1600s a new, more scientific view of the world had been taking hold all over Europe. By the 1700s educated people from Italy to England were devoting themselves to the study of physics, chemistry, and natural history.

The advances made in science had a widespread influence. Throughout the Middle Ages most people had been content to accept on faith what the Church taught about the nature of things. Now, more and more, people began to adopt a more scientific view: They began to trust their own powers of observation and of reasoning. Faith in the

The intimate gatherings of the well-to-do, known as salons, played an important role in the spread of the new ideas of the Enlightenment. There the men and women of Parisian society mingled regularly with the philosophes. The drawing above shows several authors who wrote for Diderot's *Encyclopedia* together at supper. The man at the center of the table is Voltaire. Diderot is to his right. *Cultural Services of the French Embassy.*

Church and its teachings began to wane. Criticisms of Church doctrines and practices became more and more common.

Along with the new belief in the powers of human reason came a growing distrust of authority. People believed they could think for themselves and resented having someone else tell them what to think or do. Antagonism toward all authority—that of kings and lords, as well as that of the Church—grew.

The ideas of the Enlightenment also included new theories about how governments ought to be run and about the role they should play in people's lives. Scientists had discovered a number of natural laws, such as the law of gravity, that governed what happened in the physical universe. People began to believe that there were also natural laws that governed or ought to govern the way a society was set up. Ideas about these laws varied, but usually they involved the belief that there were certain natural rights to which all men and women were entitled. It was the job of government to see that a nation was run in harmony with natural law and safeguard people's natural rights.

The new ideas of the Enlightenment were put forth by a group of men known as "philosophes." The philosophes were not scholars or university men. Often they were more popularizers of new ideas than they were original thinkers. They came from all walks of life, and most spent much of their time either at salons or writing for the general public. They were a varied and colorful group.

"Monarchy is an abnormal condition that always degenerates into despotism."

So spoke the fictional, opinionated Persian traveler named Usbek, in one of the most popular books of the early 1700s. To illustrate his point, Usbek told the tale of the Troglodytes, an imaginary people from Arabia. A small group of the Troglodytes had for some time been able to achieve a remarkably harmonious and flourishing society without benefit of a monarch, simply by their dedication to living virtuous lives. As their numbers increased the people decided they ought to have a king. But with a king to tell them what to do, they soon lost that individual dedication to virtue, and with it their happiness and prosperity.

Usbek, with his Troglodyte story, was in reality voicing the conviction of the great eighteenth-century philosophe Charles-Louis Montesquieu, whose creation he was. Usbek and his companion Rica were the main characters in Montesquieu's first important work, *The Persian Letters*. Basically a satirical look at contemporary French society through the eyes of these two Persian travelers, the book contains the germ of Montesquieu's political ideas. Chief among these was the belief that despotism, or tyrannical rule, stripped a people of its virtue, integrity, and happiness.

The Persian Letters sold like hotcakes and quickly made its author a kind of underground hero. Before its publication the Baron de Montesquieu had been content to live the quiet life of a provincial nobleman and lawyer. Shortly afterward Montesquieu left his Bordeaux home for several years of adventure. He traveled widely, enjoyed Paris salon life, and even developed a reputation for loose living. But he never abandoned his study of liberty and government. Even his travels were used to make extensive notes on the governments of other nations. "Study," he once said, "has been for me the sovereign remedy against all the disappointments of life. I have never known any trouble that an hour's reading would not dissipate."

Throughout his works Montesquieu was concerned with how people might be protected from the threat of despotism. His masterwork, *The Spirit of the Laws*, put forth the theory that by separating the various branches of a government a nation could protect itself against any one branch becoming too powerful. This theory of the separation of powers had a strong influence on the drafters of the American Constitution.

Montesquieu was not a radical. His description of the virtuous, self-governing society of the Troglodytes was designed to be inspirational, not practical. But he also remarked that "pure air is sometimes harmful to those who have lived in swampy miasma." Many people, he conceded, were not ready for such complete liberty and responsibility. For his fellow Frenchmen and -women, he thought a limited monarchy was the wisest kind of government.

"Crush the infamous thing!"

With these famous words another well-known philosophe, François-Marie Arouet de Voltaire, struck out at a different kind of tyranny—that of intolerance, of suppression of freedom of thought. The "infamous thing" he was referring to was the Church, which he saw as especially intolerant of any ideas not in accord with its own.

Voltaire's life spanned the eighteenth century. Born in 1694, he died in 1778 at the age of eighty-four. For many of those years he devoted himself to fighting intolerance of all kinds—superstition, fanaticism, censorship, as well as religious oppression.

Voltaire's weapon was his pen. Although his father had wanted him to go into law, Voltaire at an early age began writing tragic plays. Never one to be wholly serious, he also wrote witty verses that satirized life at Court. It was not long before his daring poetry landed him in the Bastille, the infamous Paris prison, and then had him exiled to England. But a prison stay could not silence him. While locked up he worked on *The Henriade*, a poem that attacked organized religion. And on his return from England he published a collection of reflections on English political and religious freedom that pointed to the lack of freedom in his own country.

His *Letters Concerning the English Nation* once again got Voltaire into trouble with the authorities. He was obliged to leave Paris and take up residence at the provincial château of a noblewoman he had befriended. No matter where he lived, Voltaire never ceased writing—pamphlets, histories, encyclopedia articles, poems, satires, essays—and always plays, which remained his favorite genre. His interests ranged from Newtonian physics to the problem of evil. "Disbelief is the foundation of all knowledge," he once remarked. No matter what his subject, Voltaire began by questioning commonly held assumptions about it. So firmly did he adhere to this principle that he has often been referred to as "the skeptic." He helped to make skepticism a basic ingredient of Enlightenment thought.

Like Montesquieu, Voltaire in his political thinking remained dubious about the possibility of genuine democracy. "As regards the people," he said, "they will always be stupid and barbarous. They are oxen who require a yoke, a goad, and some hay." The philosopher had himself added the noble name "de Voltaire" to his bourgeois surname "Arouet," and he generally preferred the company of the upper classes. To Voltaire, not all men were suited for full freedom. He, too, saw limited monarchy as the sort of government best suited to France.

"Man is born free; and everywhere he is in chains."

This tribute to man's natural goodness was voiced by a third giant of the Enlightenment, Jean-Jacques Rousseau. Rousseau was the first of the philosophes to sing the praises of the common man, and in doing so stood in marked contrast to Voltaire and Montesquieu. He was a true democrat, and, of all the philosophes, Rousseau had the most radical ideas. "All the first impulses of nature are good and right," he wrote. Rousseau believed that all men were innately good, whatever their social origin. He himself was of a humble background—the son of a Swiss watchmaker who all his life felt himself an outsider. Rousseau maintained, on principle, a simple lifestyle and shunned the luxury so popular at the time. In Paris, even at the height of his fame, he lived in a modest, two-room apartment and supported himself copying music.

Rousseau believed passionately in the importance of individual freedom. And because of his faith in the basic goodness of all people, he believed freedom was something any man could handle.

But Rousseau believed just as passionately in the importance of cooperation, of aligning one's self-interest with that of one's society. "Man's proper study is that of his relationships," he wrote. "Our sweetest existence is relative and collective." For Rousseau, freedom was not simply the license to do what one wanted. A man's freedom had to be used to better his society if he were to know true happiness.

This idea—that the state, its preservation and welfare, should be of supreme importance to all men—was one of Rousseau's most important contributions to the thinking of the age. The work in which it was most fully developed was *The Social Contract.*

It was more than just Rousseau's ideas that were bold and original. The very tone of his writing inaugurated a new era. "The man who has lived the most is not he who has counted most years, but he who has felt most life," he once said. In a bold departure from the "cult of reason" that had dominated the century, Rousseau asserted that the development of a man's heart, of his ability to feel, was more important than the formation of his intellect. His own writings— passionate, emotional, personal—were a testimony to this belief. They stood in stark contrast to the dry wit of Voltaire and the classic logic of Montesquieu. Many of those who read his novels or other works found their whole outlook on life changed by them.

How influential were the ideas of the philosophes? Certainly they had a wider and more immediate impact than had many new ideas in past ages. In part this was due to the growth of salons in Paris, where the new theories and the men whose writings popularized them became a central attraction in chic society. But it was also due to the growth, for the first time in history, of a sizable reading public. The publishing business had grown steadily throughout the 1700s. Book production had expanded tremendously. The 1700s were, among other things, the great age of encyclopedias. The first and greatest of these to be produced was Denis Diderot's *Encyclopedia,* a work whose goal was "to bring together all the knowledge scattered over the face of the earth." The project took nearly thirty years to complete, and ran to thirty-five large volumes. Similar multivolume projects soon followed.

The number of newspapers and journals had also grown. In 1700 there were three periodical publications in France. By 1765 there were nineteen. And the number continued to rise. By the time of the Revolution most cities and large towns had their own papers.

Books and journals were still expensive. A single issue of a journal might cost a workingman in the provinces two weeks' wages. However, there were soon many reading rooms and public libraries where people could pay a modest annual fee and find all the latest books and journals.

The salons of well-to-do society were no longer the only place where new ideas were discussed. Arthur Young, an Englishman staying in Paris at the time, was amazed by the debates in the bourgeois coffee houses, which he referred to as "singular and astonishing spectacles":

. . . They are not only crowded within, but other expectant crowds are at the doors and windows, listening (with mouths hanging open) to certain orators, who from chairs or tables harangue each his little audience. The eagerness with which they are heard, and the thunder of applause they receive for every sentiment of more than common hardiness or violence against the present government, cannot easily be imagined. I am all amazement at the ministry permitting such nests and hotbeds of sedition and revolt, which disseminate amongst the people, every hour, principles that by and by must be opposed with vigour. . . .

Dozens of cafés such as those Young described flourished under the arcades of the grand structure known as the Palais Royal.

Many French people were still traditional and conservative in their thinking. Still, the new ideas did play a decisive role in shaping the thinking that led to a new France. When confronted with the repeated failures and mistakes of the existing government, it was a simple step for such people to propose overhauling it—along the lines proposed by the philosophes.

The Growth of the Financial Crisis

The financial crisis that hit France in the 1760s and 1770s was the spark that ignited the long fuse of tensions that had built up in the nation. All the tensions that existed in France in the later 1700s— the frictions among and within the various orders of society, the ferment caused by the new ideas of the Enlightenment—might never have built to the point of explosion and revolution had it not been for the financial crisis.

Between 1730 and 1785 France fought a number of foreign wars that cost the nation millions of livres. These wars, which involved a struggle with England for dominance in the colonies, included the French and Indian Wars, with which students of American history are familiar. In order to pay off its debts, the nation borrowed heavily. Naturally the government looked to taxes as the means of raising the necessary funds.

When Louis XVI became king in 1774, he knew that some kind of drastic reform of the nation's tax system was necessary if the country were to survive. He appointed as finance ministers two able men. Jacques Turgot, a capable if tactless administrator who was familiar with the latest economic theories, was followed by Jacques Necker, a quiet Protestant Swiss banker and self-made millionaire reputed to be a financial genius.

The Revolt of the Nobility

But both Turgot's and Necker's ideas met with great resistance on the part of the nobility. Many members of the second estate had already begun to feel they were losing their privileged position to the growing ranks of the newly ennobled. The reforms now contemplated might do away with their cherished tax-exempt status as well. Throughout the provinces nobles appealed to the ancient regional courts, the *parlements*. According to an old custom dating back to times when the French king was much less powerful and the nation's feudal lords much more so, the *parlements* had the right to refuse to support any edict of the king they believed to be unjust.

The nobles' protest had the desired effect. Louis XVI dismissed first Turgot, then Necker. Louis then chose as finance minister Alexander de Calonne. In 1786 Calonne presented a proposal for reform that was truly forward-thinking and definitely threatening to noble privilege. It included taxes that would be levied on all landowners, re-gardless of class or status. It also included plans for new local governing bodies to replace the old *parlements*. These new bodies would be composed of men from all orders and would be closely supervised by agents of the king.

Knowing that the *parlements* were not likely to approve Calonne's plan, Louis summoned a special group of representatives of the three estates, an Assembly of Notables. But they, too, registered violent opposition. Besides, the Notables stressed that only another ancient governing body, the Estates General, could approve taxes. Louis dismissed both the Notables and his third finance minister. Reluctantly, the King approached the *Parlement* of Paris, the most powerful of all the local *parlements*, to ask for its approval of the new proposals. The *Parlement* approved some of the new measures but refused to grant approval to the more controversial ones, such as the new land tax to be imposed on all landowners. For these, it said—as had the Notables—approval of the Estates General was required.

Since the Middle Ages, France had had a representative governing body whose function was similar to that of the *parlements*, but which, like England's Parliament, represented all the subjects of the realm. This body, the Estates General, was composed of representatives of all three estates—clergy, nobility, and commoners. Its function was to approve measures put forth by the king. In earlier centuries, the Estates General had had some power. However, it did not meet regularly, and once the kings of France began to gain in power, it was not summoned at all. The last time the body had met was in 1614. Now the nation's nobles were calling for it to meet again.

Louis refused. Not only did he refuse to summon the Estates General, he also struck out at the *parlements* by issuing new royal edicts designed to destroy their power. At this the nobility revolted. In the spring of 1788 violence broke out in several cities.

After several months, on July 5, 1788, the King relented and agreed to summon the Estates General. To the nobles of France it seemed as if victory were indeed at hand. They had had their way with the King. They also felt confident that when the Estates General convened, that body would usher in an era of reform that would crush the King's absolute power and would restore to their order the power it had enjoyed in days of old. Of course, new rights for the bourgeoisie or lower taxes for the poor had no place in their plans.

"What Is the Third Estate?"

The revolution that began in the spring of 1788 began as a revolution of the nobility. By spring of 1789, however, it would be transformed into a revolution of the bourgeoisie.

The nobility had looked ahead confidently to the meeting of the Estates General because they intended to insist that it be composed and conducted in the same way in which it had been when it last met in 1614. At that time each estate had had the same number of representatives. Also, each estate had voted as a body, casting a single vote. Since it could be counted on that neither of the first two estates would favor new taxes that would affect them, and since each estate was required to vote as a block, casting a single ballot, the third estate was bound to lose out on such questions.

On September 25, 1788, the Parlement of Paris publicly announced the edict of the King, that the Estates General were to meet in May of the following year. However, the Parlement, composed chiefly of the noble magistrates of the city, went a step further. It added to the edict that the Estates should meet in the same manner in which they had in 1614.

Not everyone, however, shared the nobles' view that the Estates General should meet in their accustomed fashion. As word spread of what the Parlement had done, and people learned what the consequences would be of meeting in the manner of 1614, members of the third estate all across the nation were incensed. Up until this point the bourgeoisie had enthusiastically joined the nobility in opposing the King and the arbitrary way in which he levied taxes. But now it looked as though they would have virtually no say in an assembly that would help to shape the future of their country. The mounting tensions between the bourgeoisie and nobles erupted.

Coffeehouses in Paris buzzed with activity. And the reading public had never been kept busier. Every day new pamphlets rolled off the presses and were quickly passed from hand to hand. Some of these concerned the debate about how the upcoming Estates General should be composed and conducted. Others looked ahead even further and put forth new ideas about how the government might be changed.

Typical of the pamphlets of this time was one entitled *What Is the Third Estate?* by the Abbé Sieyès. Emmanuel-Joseph Sieyès was a man who had entered the Church only at his parents' insistence, and who had devoted much of his time in seminary to studying political philosophy. Sieyès cared deeply about the poor, but his slight build and weak voice made him an ineffectual spokesperson for their plight. When he turned to writing in 1788, he at last found his niche.

"What is the third estate?" asked Sieyès in what was to become the most widely read pamphlet of the time. "Everything," was his categorical answer. "What has it been heretofore in the political order?" the pamphlet continued. "Nothing. What does it demand? To become something therein."

Sieyès' pamphlet expanded on this bold beginning to argue that the third estate was in fact the nation itself and, because of this, should have as many representatives at the meeting of the Estates General as the other two estates combined.

Copies of the new pamphlets were sent to the provinces, and soon political ferment had spread far beyond Paris. All across France men who came to be called "Patriots" held debates about the upcoming Estates General, about the dangers a privileged class caused the nation. Petitions urging the King to permit double representation for the third estate began to pour into the capital, sometimes as many as eight hundred in a week. Now it was the bourgeoisie that was up in arms.

The first victory for the bourgeois revolutionaries came at the very end of 1788. On December 27 the King declared that the third estate would have double the number of representatives at the meeting of the Estates General. However, it still was an open question whether the voting would be by head (each representative getting one vote) or by order (a single vote for each estate).

Elections and Grievances

The atmosphere was charged as 1789 rolled in and the long process of electing delegates to the Estates General began. For the first four months local assemblies of nobles, clergy, and commoners across the nation met to elect their delegates to the May meeting. At the same time the three orders were conducting elections, they were also, at the invitation of the King, drawing up lists of grievances, or injustices, they wanted addressed at the Estates General. These lists were called "cahiers." By the time they were completed there was a surprising amount of agreement among the cahiers of the three orders. Nearly all included a condemnation of the King's absolute power (although they did not condemn the monarchy itself). Most expressed a desire for regular meetings of the Estates General to vote on taxes and approve new laws. A call for reforms in the Church was a common grievance. Most also included demands for a constitution, for individual liberty, and for freedom of the press. There was even significant agreement about the future of noble privilege. Most of the cahiers of the third estate opposed the continuation of noble privilege. But, surprisingly, so did many of those of the second estate. Less than ten percent of the nobles' cahiers specifically called for preservation of noble distinctions! Clearly, change was in the air.

As deputies across the nation prepared for the trip to Versailles, Frenchmen and -women of all orders looked forward to the meeting of the estates as an opportunity to make changes that were long past due.

The question of how voting in the Estates General would be handled, however, was still undecided.

The Estates General opened on May 5, 1789, in the vast hall of the Hôtel des Menus-Plaisirs, at Versailles. Louis presided over the proceedings from his throne. The principal speech of the day, describing the nation's economic situation, was so long that Jacques Necker, the finance minister, needed an assistant to help him read it. *French Embassy Press and Information Division.*

The Estates General Are Convened

May 5, 1789, was set as the day on which the proceedings of the Estates General would officially begin. Louis XVI sat solemnly at the end of the great Hall of Mirrors as, one after another, the delegates of the first estate filed in. The parish priests were dressed in plain black habits, the bishops in their splendid robes. Once they were all assembled, the King officially welcomed them. Next to walk proudly down the length of the great hall were the delegates of the nobility. There was a rustle of silk and satin as they came in, their shiny swords glistening in the light, the billowing plumes on their hats bobbing gently. The nobles, too, were all officially received.

They were not, however, followed by the representatives of the third estate. These men in their plain black suits were considered too lowly in status to be greeted in the Hall of Mirrors. Instead, the King retired to a more modest room. There, after he kept them waiting for three hours, he had the delegates of the common people file past him. There was a deep silence as the gentlemen in black slowly walked past, for the King said not so much as a "good morning" to any of them, save one older gentleman who looked fairly harmless.

Several days later the meetings began. After the manner of the 1614 convention each of the orders was expected to meet separately, in the quarters assigned to it, to examine the credentials of its delegates. The clergy retired to their hall, the nobility to theirs.

But the delegates of the third estate remained in the large hall in which the grand opening had taken place. They insisted that the three orders meet together and the credentials of each delegate be examined by the whole convention. They feared that any separation of the estates would lead to vote by order. Until the King granted their request, they refused to budge.

Setting the Scene:
The Palace at Versailles

The palace had accommodations for three thousand courtiers and for many more servants. There was also a single room used to house a special clock, another magnificent room built just for the King's throne, a room for the gilt-draped royal billiard table, and a room for the King's dogs with a separate niche for each. While many people would consider having their own bedroom a luxury, the King and Queen of France each had a whole suite of rooms.

When King Louis XIV began work on the old hunting lodge of his father, Louis XIII, he dreamed of making it the most magnificent dwelling in the world. In large measure he succeeded. He hired the best architects, artists, and artisans of his time. At one point, twenty-two thousand workmen and six thousand horses were working on the reconstruction. These artists, architects, and workmen worked on Versailles for nearly fifty years.

The result was a royal residence grand beyond belief. Viewed from the outside, Versailles's vast redbrick facades, hundreds of high, arched windows, and wide marble steps created an air of stately grandeur. The interior was more magnificent still.

The Hall of Mirrors, where Louis XVI received delegates to the Estates General, was three quarters the length of a football field and over forty feet high. It was decorated with rich marble, gilded sculpture, and more than three hundred Venetian mirrors. At night these reflected the light from fourteen silver and crystal chandeliers. For grand occasions the hall was lined with orange trees in silver tubs.

The Hall of Mirrors was just one of many grand salons that were used by the King for a variety of purposes. All were rich in marble, gilt, and statues sculpted by the most renowned artists of the time. The private rooms of the royal family were also imposing. Furniture was covered with enamel, silver, and gilt. High ceilings were decorated with masterpieces of the painters' art.

The grandeur of the palace was continued in its gardens. The elaborate formal gardens of Versailles covered two hundred fifty acres. They were crisscrossed by miles of straight, wide pathways and avenues bordered by precisely pruned hedges and rows of flowers planted just so. These pathways divided the gardens into dozens of small glens and groves. Each of these was decorated with special trees and statues to give it a unique appearance. Fourteen hundred fountains dotted the gardens. Each year tens of thousands of annual plants were put in and, as soon as the weather permitted, three thousand exotic trees accustomed to southern climates were brought out from a special greenhouse called the Orangerie.

The vastness, precision, and stateliness of the formal gardens seemed to encourage dignified strolling with the head held high. In fact, Versailles as a whole was a symbol of a way of life characterized by great formality, artifice, and extravagance.

Day after day the deputies milled about, engaging in earnest talk and hot debates as they got acquainted with one another. All about them pressed crowds of local citizens who were granted free admittance and who applauded and booed the many speakers. But despite all this seeming activity, the proceedings of the Estates General remained at a standstill, unable even to open until either the King or the commoners gave way.

The bold Abbé Sieyès at last ended the contest of wills. "Cutting the cable" was what was called for, he declared. Since, as he had written in his famous pamphlet, the third estate *was* the nation, Sieyès proposed that the representatives of the third estate declare themselves the representative body of France—whether the King approved or not. Representatives of the other two orders would be invited formally to join the commoners. His proposal was accepted. A formal roll was set up, on which members of the clergy and nobility who accepted the invitation could sign their names. For several days no one signed. But by June 16 the names of nineteen priests had been entered.

Heartened by this sign of support, Sieyès then proposed that the third estate choose a new name to indicate the new role it had created for itself. A day of bedlam followed. Often several dozen delegates were on their feet at once, each debating one or another of various proposed names. Others crowded around them, pushing and shoving for a turn to climb onto the rostrum. Finally, on June 17, the crowds quieted. The name "National Assembly" was up for a vote. The count came in at 491 in favor, 89 opposed. Someone leaned out a window to announce the numbers to those outdoors, and crowds both in and outside the hall cheered wildly. In their eyes, France now had a new governing body—the National Assembly.

The Tennis Court Oath

Not so in the eyes of the King and Queen, however. The following day when the commoners returned to their hall, they found the doors locked. The actions of the third estate were illegal, Louis declared, and its meetings could not continue.

But locked doors were not enough to break the will of the new Assembly. In no time the delegates had moved the meeting to a nearby indoor tennis court someone had suggested might be vacant. There, in a large room furnished with nothing but a bench and an armchair, amid a whirl of noise and confusion, one of the delegates rose and raised his voice. The others fell silent as he proposed that they all take an oath never to separate until an acceptable constitution had been established. In little time the delegates were all, with the single exception of Martel d'Auch of Castelnaudary, coming forward, arms raised in salute, to take the oath.

It was not long before word of the Tennis Court Oath reached the King. Louis knew he had to take action. He called a meeting of all three estates for June 23. There he declared himself willing to grant the delegates some of their requests, such as gaining the consent of the nation's representatives for any new taxes and taking steps to establish a free press. But he still insisted that the three orders be kept separate. He also insisted that there be no reforms other than those he himself granted.

Such token concessions failed to satisfy the members of the new

The Tennis Court Oath, in which every member of the new National Assembly save one (arms crossed, in the lower right-hand corner) pledged to remain together until a constitution had been drafted, was immortalized by the famous painting of Jacques Louis David. The drawing for it is shown above. David, one of the great artists of the revolutionary years, was a passionate revolutionist and intimately involved with the political subjects he painted. The revolutionary government tapped his artistic genius to design new "national costumes" and to create the staging for Robespierre's Festival of the Supreme Being. *SCALA/Art Resource, Inc.*

National Assembly. When at the end of the meeting the commoners were ordered by the King to disperse, they defiantly refused to leave. "We are here by the will of the people and . . . we shall not stir from our seats unless forced to do so by bayonets," declared one of the representatives.

Upon hearing a report that the delegates were still in the hall, the King heaved a heavy sigh. "Well, damn it, let them stay," he said.

He felt beaten at last. On June 27 he ordered all representatives of the clergy and nobility who had not already done so to join with the commoners in the new National Assembly. The revolt of the bourgeoisie, so it seemed, had met with success.

But this victory was only the beginning of a much larger revolt. For the time being the middle classes were content. But how long would that last? And what about the rest of the third estate?

The Revolt Spreads to the Lower Classes

Every day the price of bread in Paris had been rising higher. The cost of a single loaf was approaching fifteen *sous* (a *sou* was a small coin worth $1/20$ of a livre)—a half day's wages for many workers. Bakers' shops were surrounded every morning by anxious crowds of people who often stood in line all day only to have the supply run out. The harvest of 1788 had been ruined by hail, and by spring there was almost no flour left.

Conditions in the rest of the country were little better. Harvests had been bad all over. Hunger and famine were widespread. In addition, wages had dropped, and thousands of men, women, and children were forced out onto the roads, where they turned to begging and pillaging simply to survive. Arthur Young, traveling not far outside Paris at the time, was so struck by one poor woman he met on the road that he devoted a whole page in his journal to her. "An Englishman who has not travelled cannot imagine the figure made by infinitely the greater part of the countrywomen in France," he wrote. "This woman, at no great distance, might have been taken for sixty or seventy, her figure was so bent, and her face so furrowed and hardened by labor; but she said she was only twenty-eight."

France had known bad times in the past. But now there was a difference. The events of 1788–89 had given the people a new target for their fears and frustrations. Throughout the countryside wild rumors spread that the famine and hard times were actually part of a plot by the aristocracy. Some said the Queen was preparing to blow up the building where the National Assembly met. Soon the fear and mistrust would reach crisis proportions.

The center of the swirling rumors and mounting tensions remained in Paris, however. Many of the beggars and brigands who roamed country roads wound up looking for work in the nation's capital. The city's winding, narrow streets swarmed with restless, suspicious men and women.

By July 11, 1789, the capital had reached a fevered pitch of excitement. It had been less than two weeks since the King had given the National Assembly his official approval. Yet word had gotten out that troops were beginning to arrive on the outskirts of Paris. Louis insisted that they were only there to protect people against the swelling crowds, but it was clear the King was up to something. The cafés were full of wild talk about what he might do.

The morning of July 12 the news broke. Louis had dismissed Jacques Necker, the liberal finance minister on whom many in the third estate had pinned their hopes for a new and fairer tax system. A penniless young lawyer named Camille Desmoulins leaped up on one of the café tables. In a wild voice he began denouncing the government. "There is not a moment to lose," he cried; "we have only one course of action—to rush to arms!" Within minutes the crowds were pouring out of the Palais Royal and into the streets of Paris. The search for arms was on.

The Fall of the Bastille

For the rest of the day and on into the night, restless mobs roamed the streets, breaking into any shop where there might be weapons to pilfer. A civic militia was formed to help keep order, but by the time July 14 dawned, overcast and gray, the crowd's desperation to find arms had reached a peak.

Early that morning word came that there were arms in the Hôtel des Invalides, a public hospital for wounded soldiers. In little time wild mobs clamored at its gates, shouting for guns. They forced their way in and streamed through the building, grabbing whatever weapons they found. All together, the rioters came away with twenty-eight thousand muskets. There was one problem, however. They had found very little powder and very few cartridges. For these, they were told, they would have to go to the Bastille.

In the center of the working-class section of Paris, rising above the jumble of roofs and chimneys, stood a huge, forbidding gray fortress with solid rock walls ten feet thick and parapets that loomed over eighty feet in height. For several hundred years it had been used as a prison for people who had been arrested not for breaking any law, but simply by order of the King. (As an absolute monarch, the King had the right to send to prison anyone he so much as suspected of disloyalty.) Prisoners arrived, it was said, in carriages with drawn blinds, and mystery surrounded much that went on inside. In fact, conditions at the Bastille in 1789 were better than those found in many Parisian prisons. Yet in the minds of the common people it was a symbol of the oppressive nature of their government.

When the incensed crowd arrived at the Bastille, the commander of the royal troops there was ready and waiting. Cannons were aimed at the surrounding streets. Piles of stones lay at the tops of the towers, ready to be hurled onto the heads of a threatening crowd. The drawbridges that separated the fortress from the land around it were up.

A delegation of the people had been admitted to talk with the commander, a timid soldier named de Launay. They had secured from him a promise that he would withdraw the guns. But the crowds were

For hundreds of years myth and mystery had surrounded the great stone fortress known as the Bastille. Horrifying stories were told of its deep dungeons and dark vaults, of prisoners kept in chains or forced to live in darkness for years on end. The close-up captures the tremendous energy with which the crowds of working people from the surrounding district at last conquered this fearsome and often-resented structure. *The Bettmann Archive.*

by this point too angry to believe in the commander's good intentions and, in any event, too noisy to hear the results of the meeting. As they saw the guns being withdrawn, they concluded that they were being loaded. Soon two men managed to climb onto the roof of a shop near the fortress wall and from there to jump down into the Bastille and slash the pulleys that held up one drawbridge. As the heavy planks crashed down, the crowd surged across the moat.

Just then the sound of shots rang through the streets.

Some claimed it was the assailants who had fired first; others, the soldiers. It did not matter. Once begun, the siege was on. Soon hundreds of the King's troops had defected to help the people's cause. Throughout the afternoon their cannons pounded against the fortress walls. Violence spread through the streets as the mobs attempted to crash the remaining drawbridge. When a peace delegation from the city arrived, the noise of the gunshots and shouts and cries was so great they could not make themselves heard.

By five in the afternoon, de Launay was urging the attackers to accept his surrender. He passed a note through a slit in the gate, threatening to blow up the Bastille if a surrender were not accepted. But when the content of the note was made known, it was greeted with jeers and continued shouts of "Down with the bridges!"

At last, wearied by it all, de Launay handed the gate key to an officer standing nearby. The officer proceeded to lower the remaining drawbridge. Immediately, the crowd rushed in and scrambled to find the barrels of powder and shot. In their frenzy they fell on the very man who had let them in; de Launay was stuck with bayonets like a pincushion. Amid pools of blood, the siege at last came to an end.

The taking of the Bastille served to reinforce the position of the third estate. Louis had in fact been amassing troops in preparation for one last attempt to destroy the National Assembly. Now all such plans were dashed. On July 15 he told the Assembly that he had ordered the troops to leave Versailles. On July 16 he restored Necker to his former position and recognized Jean Sylvain Bailly as the mayor of a new citizens' government of Paris.

Initiative in the Revolution had clearly passed from the nobility to the bourgeoisie. The taking of the Bastille indicated that the common people would also play an important role. In addition, this victory of the people set a precedent for resorting to violence and bloodshed in the name of justice and the Revolution. To what might this lead? The question would be answered soon enough, for the march of events was moving steadily forward.

2

Chronology

1789

July–August	the Great Fear
August 4	start of abolition of feudalism
August 27	Declaration of the Rights of Man and the Citizen
October 5–6	march on Versailles
November 2	Church property nationalized

•

1790

	drafting of new constitution
July 12	Civil Constitution of the Clergy passed
July 14	The Festival of the Fédération
fall	growing dissension among clergy
November 27	decree requiring civic oath for clergy

Chapter Two:

The National Assembly Reforms the Nation

To the French peasantry, the world was a fearsome place. Even young children were introduced at an early age to the harsh realities of life. The heroes of French fairy tales had to resort constantly to wily schemes in order to keep the gangs of bandits, wolves, and other forces of evil at bay. In our version of "Jack and the Beanstalk," the giant with his "fee fie fo fums" is a jovial character, and Jack is able to get his bag of gold simply by waiting for him to fall asleep. In the French version, the giant is a cruel, cunning monster. To defeat him, "petit Jean" must torture him in his sleep and trick the giant's wife and daughter into baking themselves to death in an oven.

The stories told to children were similar to those adults heard from one another. There were constantly tales of spreading plagues, threatening barbarian invaders, approaching famine. And these disasters were never seen as chance occurrences, but rather as vicious plots. For the rural French, the devil was real and his agents were everywhere.

To people accustomed to believing such myths and rumors, it didn't take much for the news of July 14 to be twisted into fantastic tales. It took several days for the story of the Bastille to reach the outlying areas of rural France. En route, passed from traveler to tavern keeper to traveler, the tale was quickly twisted. The victory of the third estate was soon blown up into announcements that the Estates General were about to do away with the tithe and other feudal dues. Most important, within a matter of days, the news from Paris had revived all the peasants' old fears about plots and robbers. Whispered tales of bands—and even armies—of brigands sent by nobles to attack peasant farms passed from village to village. Some of these stories were even printed in local papers. Within a week of the Bastille's fall, violence had erupted all over France.

Dozens of châteaux were sacked, and some burned. Feudal papers that detailed the many dues and obligations peasants owed their lords were tossed gleefully onto huge bonfires. Manorial forests and fish ponds were devastated; the homes deserted by frightened lords were looted and stripped. For several weeks these gory tales of rural violence were commonplace all over France.

In a vicious spiral that came to be known as the Great Fear, the violence, which had grown out of fear, led to still more fear, and this in turn to more violence. It was not long before stories of this activity filtered back to Paris. The deputies grew increasingly alarmed. Something had to be done.

Obligations of a Typical Peasant in the Ancien Régime

FINANCIAL OBLIGATIONS

aides: excise tax on such goods as wines, playing cards, soaps

capitation: poll (head) tax

cens: fixed land rent (usually not very high)

champart: land rent, usually heavy—$1/8$ of a farmer's crops

fees for the upkeep of the lord's pigeons

fees for the use of the manorial mill, bakery, and winepress

gabelle: salt tax

lods et ventes: sales tax charged when land changed hands

taille: basic tax of the *ancien régime,* based on income

tithe: annual sum paid to the Church, traditionally $1/10$ of a farmer's crops and dairy produce but in fact averaging $1/13$

tolls on manorial roads

traites et douanes: customs duties, exacted whenever a person crossed one of the many provincial and other territorial boundaries within France

vingtième: kind of income tax, originally set at 5%

SERVICE OBLIGATIONS

allowing the lord to hunt on one's land

corvée: performance of work on the nation's roads, or the lending of carts for use by the military

Since July 14 the members of the National Assembly had been meeting in their quarters at Versailles, debating how to begin drafting a constitution. But by the beginning of August, debate centered instead around how to stop the violence in the countryside. At first the representatives could only think of sending in troops to restore order. But a group of deputies from Brittany had another idea: Give the peasants what they wanted—do away with feudal privilege.

In recent years the yoke of the peasants' obligations had grown particularly heavy. In many areas local manor lords, trying to reassert power they feared they were losing to the rising bourgeoisie, had insisted on collecting dues that had long been ignored. In one village in Franche-Comté, on France's eastern border, the peasants' feudal obligations amounted to sixty-two livres—over half their annual income. Old obligations such as the payment of a fee for the right to have a marriage or burial were also revived, and rules that had been relaxed for years about such things as the lord's right to hunt on peasants' land were once more being strictly enforced.

To abolish dues and obligations to which many nobles now seemed to cling more fiercely than ever seemed nearly impossible. The Breton deputies had a plan, however.

"What a nation, what glory, what an honor to be a Frenchman!":
The Night of August 4

"The people are trying to shake off a yoke that has weighed on their shoulders for many centuries; it must be admitted, gentlemen, that this insurrection, though blameworthy insofar as any form of violence is blameworthy, can be excused by the sheer misery to which the people have been subjected." So spoke not a rural deputy, but the Duke d'Aiguillon, one of the richest noblemen in France. The Duke followed his plea with a proposal for action: He would give up his feudal rights and rents, and hoped his fellow nobles would follow suit. Satisfying the demands of the peasants, he urged, was the solution to the unrest of the countryside.

D'Aiguillon sat down to a roar of applause. Then one by one, others among the deputies rose to follow his example. Clergy gave up their claim to the tithe, nobles their hunting and fishing rights, wealthy bourgeois the special exemptions of their towns. Before long the meeting was caught up in a frenzy of self-sacrifice that went till the wee hours of the morning. So many wanted to speak that they had to stand in line; the person recording the proceedings could not write fast enough to keep up.

On August 4 France had been a feudal country, but by the dawn of August 5 it was well on its way to becoming a new nation—one in which all citizens were subject to the same laws, paid the same taxes, and were eligible for the same offices.

"What a nation, what glory, what an honor to be a Frenchman!" wrote one bourgeois delegate. Commoner and nobleman were one in celebrating the late-night session.

In the week following, the declarations of that famous night were hammered into formal decrees. By August 11 the Assembly had passed measures abolishing all personal privileges; doing away with serfdom, a system that tied peasants to their lords, and many of the dues directly connected with it; making the nation's system of justice free and equal for everyone; making public offices and positions in the army open to all; and doing away with the tithe and other church dues. The final version of the decrees was not as generous as the declarations of August 4; some of the deputies had misgivings about their spontaneous late-night sacrifices and made provision to be reimbursed for some of the dues that would be abolished. Still, the decrees of August 11 remain a revolutionary and generous-hearted document. In the course of a single week, feudalism had been largely laid to rest.

"Men are born free":
The Declaration of the Rights of Man
and the Citizen

The actions of the Assembly in early August helped to bring calm to the nation. The delegates were now able to resume their work of writing a constitution. Before getting down to the actual constitution, however, most members of the Assembly felt it was necessary first to draft an official document establishing the rights the new government would be designed to protect. They wanted everything the Assembly did to be tied to these all-important rights.

For two weeks debates raged in the Assembly's chambers. By August 27 the delegates had agreed on a draft. It was short—just seventeen articles—but its language was noble and clear, its message inspiring and strong.

"Men are born and remain free and equal in rights." This first article sets forth one of the main themes of the Declaration: the principle of equality. Many of the later articles are concerned with the specifics of the rights all were to enjoy—freedom of speech, ownership of property, equal treatment under the law.

"The source of all sovereignty is essentially in the nation." This is the second key point of the Declaration: that henceforth the people, not the king, would be the seat of all power and authority. The delegates believed that if they compromised on this at all and shared authority with the king, they could not guarantee the rights they held so dear.

". . . Inalienable rights . . . born free. . . ." In places the Declaration often reminds readers of the American Declaration of Independence or the Bill of Rights (submitted to Congress that same year). Despite the similarities, it would be inaccurate to say the French was inspired by the American. Both were international documents inspired by the best of Enlightenment thought in France, England, and America.

"We want bread!":
The October Days

The August 4 decrees and the Declaration of the Rights of Man and the Citizen won scores of enthusiastic converts to the Revolution. There was, however, one major obstacle ahead: The King refused to give the new laws his official sanction.

News of the King's resistance did not sit well with the people of Paris. The agitated mood of that city had scarcely changed since late spring. The price of bread was still high, and the lines at bakeries grew longer by the day. Unemployment was worse than ever; the streets were thronged with out-of-work artisans, valets, and small tradesmen. In cafés, red-faced speakers stirred the crowds with loud condemnations of the King and the "aristos." It would not take much to rouse the people to action.

The Declaration of the Rights of Man and the Citizen was a relatively short document—consisting of just seventeen articles. Beautiful copies were reproduced and given places of honor in Jacobin clubs across the nation. Students coming of age in revolutionary times frequently committed it to memory. *Cultural Services of the French Embassy.*

The economy of French colonies in the West Indies was dependent on the labor of African slaves. Throughout the Revolution the status of slaves in the colonies was a point of controversy. Although the first revolutionary government, the National Assembly, did not resolve the issue, later on the National Convention granted the slaves their freedom. Eventually the French colony of Haiti came to be governed by a talented former slave, Pierre Dominique Toussaint L'Ouverture. *Cultural Services of the French Embassy.*

In late September news came that the King had summoned his Flanders regiment to Versailles. In Paris rumors began to fly: Surely the King was plotting a counterrevolution.

Despite the unrest in the streets, on the night of October 1 the carriages of the great nobles of the court gathered for a gala banquet celebrating the newly arrived regiment. The boxes of the Royal Opera House were filled with rustling silks and heads resplendent with elaborate curls. After many rounds of good wine, the nobles' true feelings about the events of the last few months came out into the open. When the King and Queen made an appearance, they were greeted with a great roar of applause. The band played old royalist tunes. Some guests shouted insults at the National Assembly.

Two days later newspapers bearing accounts of the royal banquet hit the streets of Paris. Before long, angry young men were leaping on tables in the coffee shops of the Palais Royal and calling for a march to Versailles.

The morning of October 5, thousands of working-class women gathered at the Hôtel de Ville, the "City Hall" of Paris. For weeks they had spent long hours standing on lines scrambling for bread for their families. Now, caught up by the agitated mood of the city, they decided to demand that the government do something. Officials at the Hôtel de Ville suggested that they take their complaint to the King himself— at Versailles.

With that, the women were off. They swarmed toward the city gates, shouting and shaking large sticks, their numbers swelling with each block they passed. Among those who joined the motley procession were citizens who were interested in far more than bread. From under some of the peasant bonnets poked faces covered with a most unusual stubbly growth: agitators disguised as fishwives hoped to use the women's demonstration to demand that the King sanction the decrees of the National Assembly and then return with them to Paris.

□   □   □

Early in the morning of October 5, 1789, a rain-drenched and impatient group of the women and men who had marched to Versailles to petition the King entered the Palace and surged through the royal residence shouting for the Queen. They raised on their pikes the heads of two of the King's guards. This drawing is not an accurate representation of the crowd, which was made up predominantly of women. *Art Resource/Lauros-Giraudon.*

Setting the Scene:
Newspapers and the Revolution

"The King plots escape! Read all about it—just two sous!" Before 1789 such cries never would have been heard on the streets of Paris. After the establishment of the new government, they became commonplace. In a matter of months the French press, just like the society it reported on, had undergone a revolution.

France had had newspapers since 1631, but until the Revolution their contents had been controlled by a strict system of censorship. No paper was allowed to be published until it had received official permission from the court. Due to these restrictions, there were only a few official papers.

By the 1780s publishers, readers, and even government officials were making a mockery of the nation's censorship system. When they could, people bought foreign newspapers rather than support the official journals. And for "scoops" about the doings at court, or for humorous portraits of government officials, there was a rapidly growing illicit press. Scores of illegal pamphlets were printed and sold—often with the police inspector knowingly looking the other way.

Demands that censorship of the press be ended were among the most common complaints in the cahiers (lists of grievances). And one of the rights that the delegates to the new National Assembly were most insistent be included in the Declaration of the Rights of Man and the Citizen was freedom of the press.

The months following the Declaration saw an explosion in French newspaper publishing. Something like two hundred fifty new papers appeared in Paris between July and December of 1789. Many of these papers folded soon after they appeared, but many others lasted.

"Stupidities of the Week"

Small (just nine by twelve inches at the very most), printed cheaply on poor paper, and without any large headline to catch a reader's eye—such was the typical paper of the Revolution. These papers were laboriously produced on primitive hand presses that could produce, at most, three thousand sheets a day. But while their physical appearance was modest, their content riveted readers to their pages. To begin with, many had clever or even scandalous titles: *The Patriotic Hen, Stupidities of the Week, The National Denouncer.*

Their contents were often in keeping with the tone set by their titles—witty, sometimes scathing, not always based in fact. Obscene language was common in a number of the papers. Commented one editor, "Anyone who appreciates frankness . . . will not blush at the *!%#&'s and *%!!@s that I insert here and there with my joys and my angers." Some papers printed news of what was happening at the National Assembly. Others were vehicles for the opinions of their editors. Still others printed clever accounts or portraits—in both prose and verse.

The editors of the new, revolutionary papers were a colorful and courageous group indeed. A number were delegates to the Assembly who founded newspapers in order to make their views on issues more widely known. Camille Desmoulins and Maximilien Robespierre both published papers of their own. Others, such as Jean-Paul Marat, achieved fame simply on the basis of their bold and original publishing. Today Marat is known as the radical "martyr" of the Revolution who was stabbed in his bath by the beautiful Charlotte Corday. But in his own day he was best known as the editor of the popular paper *Friend of the People.*

Journalists played a key role in involving the general public in the political affairs of the nation. Even in remote villages, new, revolutionary papers read aloud after Sunday Mass kept hundreds of thousands of peasants abreast of the latest from Paris. As the Revolution progressed and violence became more commonplace, writers were often blamed for the course events were taking.

In fact, so influential was the press at this time that the Revolutionary government itself eventually felt the need to place restrictions on what editors could publish.

But a precedent had been set that could not ever be reversed entirely. Courageous editors risked their lives—and some, in fact, went to the guillotine—for daring to publish their views of what the government was doing. Freedom of the press remained an ideal the French would always cherish. Even today, French papers such as *Le Canard Enchaîné* (*The Chained Duck*) continue a tradition of outspokenness that can be traced back to the era of the Revolution.

As the day wore on, rain began to fall. Still the marchers trudged onward, chanting "Bread! Bread!" and raising their pikes, scythes, and large sticks in defiance. Their numbers had risen to six thousand. By five P.M. they had reached Versailles. Members of the National Assembly attempted to quiet the angry mob, but their attempts were in vain. "We don't give a hoot about order," they shouted. "We want bread."

That evening, the King agreed to meet with six of the women. "You know my heart," Louis told them. "I will order all the bread in Versailles to be collected and given to you." Once they had the King's promise in writing, the crowd appeared to be satisfied.

But the King's relief would be very short-lived, for within hours yet another group of marchers arrived at Versailles: twenty thousand National Guardsmen under the command of the Marquis de Lafayette, the handsome young soldier who had helped to lead the American colonists to victory over the British and who now was pouring his energies into the revolutionary cause in his own country. Sent out earlier that day along with two delegates from the government in Paris, the Guardsmen had come to ensure that the King was brought back to that city.

At eleven in the evening, despite urgings from the Queen and others that he flee, Louis met with the delegates and heard their request. He begged for permission to make his decision in the morning.

As the night wore on, ministers fleeing in fine coaches galloped past half-dressed washerwomen wringing the rain from their soaked skirts. Liveried guards and mud-spattered marchers alike sought shelter from the weather. But the uneasy peace would not last long. In the morning a group of women found a gate leading to the royal courtyard unlocked. In no time, they were at the Queen's bedroom door.

"Death to the Austrian! We'll wring her neck!" they shouted, banging at the door. Marie Antoinette sprang from her bed, threw a cape over her underclothes, and fled for the King's chambers and safety just in time. Lafayette and the National Guard managed to contain the violence, but it was clear that the crowd would not be satisfied until the King addressed the people and agreed to their demands.

Later that morning Louis stepped solemnly out onto a balcony overlooking the courtyard where the people were gathered. He was accompanied by his wife who, despite her tousled hair and hastily drawn-on dressing gown, had managed to regain her sense of dignity. "My friends," he announced, "I will go to Paris with my wife and my children."

Characters in the Revolutionary Drama:
Lafayette

While others considered it a great honor to be able to participate in the King's levée, or morning ritual, by handing him an appointed garment, the young Marquis de Lafayette saw it as a tedious obligation and got out of it whenever he could. Indeed, there was much about the life of a young nobleman the Marquis would rather have done without.

Then, as a young army officer, Lafayette happened to be present at a conversation between a British duke and several French officers. There he heard talk of a declaration of independence being written by the colonists in America. All of a sudden, years' worth of annoyances at the emptiness of aristocratic life came to a head. His imagination was fired as never before. With the air of a medieval knight pledging himself to defend his lady's honor, Lafayette resolved to devote himself to defending the noble cause of liberty. When the American general George Washington made his request for help from abroad, Lafayette lost no time in preparing for the voyage.

His devotion to the cause of liberty would continue all his life. But as strong as his passion for the rights of every man was his conviction that people needed order, peace, and stability. Lafayette had been born into a noble family of impressive credentials—his full name was Marie-Joseph-Paul-Yves-Roch-Gilbert de Motier, Marquis de Lafayette. He had been raised always to behave in a mannerly and tactful fashion, never to speak of others in anything but a kind and gracious way. This aristocratic love of order and peace never left him.

The young officer's years in America helped to give shape and weight to his ideals. For two years he fought side by side with ordinary Americans. His respect for ordinary citizens grew deeper than ever. But he was also learning the value of reasonable discussion and negotiation. In more than one instance it was only Lafayette's tact that prevented a major rift between French and American forces.

When Lafayette returned to France, he was dedicated to seeing the principles of American liberty transplanted to his own country. At first the young Marquis basked in the spillover of his

American triumph. He had played an instrumental role in the defeat of the British at Yorktown. Now, back in Paris, he was rapidly promoted and honored wherever he went. In 1788, when the French movement for liberty began, Lafayette quickly moved into a leadership role. When the National Assembly decided it needed a National Guard to keep order and to watch over the King, they chose Lafayette to head it.

As long as he perceived that the cause of liberty and the cause of public order were one and the same, Lafayette would remain a leader. But that would not be for long. Early on during the course of the Revolution, Lafayette began to grow distrustful of the crowds. Beginning with the taking of the Bastille, he saw how uncontrollable and violent they could be. In situations such as the October 1789 march on Versailles, Lafayette used his famous tact to prevent the angry crowds from getting out of hand and doing harm to the royal family. But more than tact was needed. He had long believed that the French, unlike the Americans, needed a king to steady them as much as they needed a constitution.

"*Motier l'un, motier l'autre* (half one, half the other)," the people said of him, playing on his surname, Motier, which is close to the French word for "half." It was not long before Lafayette found himself mistrusted by both the King, whom he continued to urge to accept the Constitution, and by the people, whom he tried to convince to support the monarchy. "Rascal, traitor, and enemy of the people," the National Assembly called him. Marie Antoinette remarked that it would be "better to perish than to be saved by Monsieur de Lafayette." But no matter what others might say or do, Lafayette never lost hope in his ideals nor the will to work for them.

His hope and his determination were put to severe tests. In 1792 Lafayette fled France. But he was too much a partisan of the cause of liberty to gain the trust of foreign monarchs. The years from 1792 to 1797 were spent in an Austrian prison, in dank cells that sometimes were little bigger than three by five feet. Yet still the Marquis did not abandon hope. "Liberty, in the midst of the violence of anarchy and so many hostile attacks, will not perish, in spite of its enemies," he wrote.

Not long after Lafayette was released, Napoleon Bonaparte restored order to France, and his successors, Louis XVIII, Charles X, and Louis Philippe, brought back the monarchy. Lafayette was faced with a new challenge—how to balance the need for public order or a king on the French throne with the need for liberty. Lafayette refused to support any ruler he did not feel truly had the people's interests at heart.

Many continued to disagree with the positions the Marquis took. Some, such as Louis Philippe, called him a "political fool." Yet Lafayette never swerved from his ideals as he saw them.

Perhaps the true measure of the man can be taken from the reception he got on his last visit to the United States, in 1824. Everywhere he went Lafayette was greeted by elaborate ceremony. Children were scrubbed and dressed to be presented to him. Old soldiers pressed forward, tears in their eyes, to shake his hand. Babies, and even towns were named for him. And he has been remembered for generations since as one of history's great friends of liberty.

By evening the royal family was being helped to settle in at the old Tuileries Palace in central Paris. They were prisoners in their own home.

Months of Peace

From the November 1789 diary of the United States Ambassador to France:

This morning I rise early and go to the Assemblée. Stay there till four, a tedious Session from which I derive a violent Headache. . . . Dine at the

Restorateur's & then return Home. Dress and go by Appointment to Club to meet the Vicomte de Noailles. He desires me to give Information about America to an unfortunate Man who desires to establish himself in that Country. . . . Take Tea and then visit Madame de Chastellux. The Vicomte de Ségur tells me that his Brother is arrived, and requests me to dine To Morrow. . . . I promise to do so. From Made. de Chastellux's go to Made. de Stahl's and sup. I give her my Opinion of the Speeches of this Morning. . . . Return Home immediately after Supper. This has been a pleasant Day.

The American ambassador's day was typical of this period. Despite the radical changes of the last few months, life in Parisian society had largely returned to normal after the arrival of the royal family. The doings of the National Assembly were merely fitted into the daily rounds of tea, supper, and salons.

Meanwhile, with order restored, the National Assembly settled down to the business of writing a constitution. The delegates had followed the King back from Versailles and by November were ensconced in the building that was to be their home for the next three and a half years—an old riding school near the Tuileries Palace known as the Manège.

The Manège

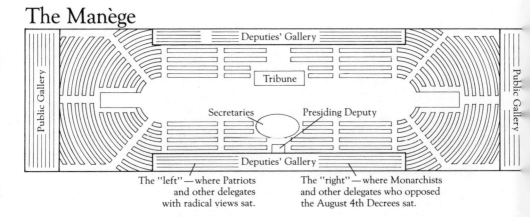

The "left"—where Patriots and other delegates with radical views sat.

The "right"—where Monarchists and other delegates who opposed the August 4th Decrees sat.

Patriots, Monarchists, Jacobins:
New Political Factions and Clubs

Although there had been remarkable unity among the delegates when they first gathered in July, it did not take long for them to fall out into several factions. The first rift occurred in the weeks following the decrees of August 4. A small group of conservative delegates opposing the August 4 decrees outright formed one faction. Other delegates, hoping to guard against the Assembly making any overly rash moves, supported the decrees but proposed that the King be given absolute veto power over any measures passed. For their support of the King they became known as the Monarchists.

The Monarchists were in the minority, however. Most of the delegates were leery of granting the King such power. Some denied that the decrees of August 11 required the King's sanction. Those who held these more radical views called themselves Patriots.

The new groups were all led by brilliant and colorful men. The spokesman for the conservatives was the Abbé Maury, an abbot of humble origins who used the colloquial speech of the common people to defend the traditional society in which he had grown up. Jean-Joseph Mounier, the handsome young lawyer from Grenoble who had first urged the delegates to take the Tennis Court Oath, led the Monarchists.

A number of men vied for leadership of the Patriot party, including several liberal members of the nobility. One of the most popular figures during the first few months was the Marquis de Lafayette, who had set the example for liberal nobles eager to break away from their background and work for change. Another early spokesman was the gruff, sometimes fearsome Honoré-Gabriel Riqueti, Comte de Mirabeau—one of the giants of the French Revolution.

When the Count entered the Manège and strode to his seat in the center rows, a hush fell over the Assembly. Delegates sitting next to him quietly moved one seat away. When he rose to speak, scanning the hall with his fiery eyes, the entire crowd fell silent.

Characters in the Revolutionary Drama: *Comte de Mirabeau*

The black-coated representatives milled around absently, their faces solemn, their voices subdued. The King had just commanded each of the three orders to retire to its separate chamber. Their hopes for a joint meeting of the Estates General were dashed. Then, from out of this hushed and somber crowd, a large man with blazing eyes came forward, his massive form shaking with rage.

"Go and tell your master that we are here by the wish of the people and that we shall not go out from here except at the point of the bayonet." With those words, the spirit of the third estate was rekindled. The man who spoke them was Honoré-Gabriel Riqueti, Comte de Mirabeau.

Less than six months later the National Assembly voted to forbid any of its delegates to serve the King as an appointed minister. One of the purposes of the motion was to tie the hands of a certain delegate who was suspected of conspiring with the Crown. The delegate against whom the legislation was aimed was the Comte de Mirabeau.

Who was this Comte de Mirabeau? Was he a friend of the people and of the Revolution, or their foe?

One of the towering figures of the Revolution, Mirabeau defies easy classification. More than almost any other, he was a man who thought for himself.

Honoré-Gabriel Riqueti was born into a noble family from southern France with a reputation both for courage on the battlefield and for scandalous behavior. As a young man Mirabeau quarreled easily, spent recklessly, and had a series of extramarital affairs. His profligate behavior gained him not only a reputation for immorality, but a series of prison sentences and banishments as well.

Honoré-Gabriel Riqueti, Comte de Mirabeau, was described by his father as "ugly as Satan." His head was abnormally large, his neck massive, and his hair a huge kinky mass. His eyes, which seemed eternally on fire, bulged from their sockets when he was angered or excited. While some found Mirabeau's appearance repulsive or frightening, many women found him strangely magnetic. *Culver Pictures, Inc.*

By 1789 Mirabeau was a man who had seen much of the world and was wise in its ways. He had definite ideas about what ailed his nation and about how things could be set right. He favored the abolition of the old feudal privileges of the nobility and the drafting of a constitution. This stand helped him to win election as a third estate delegate to the Estates General, despite his noble background.

Mirabeau quickly became a leader of the third estate delegates. In large measure this was due to his great power as a speaker. "His voice was full, manly, and sonorous," said one who heard him. He was the first in the Assembly to dare to speak without a prepared text. When he took the floor, whether to read a speech or to speak extemporaneously, he often brought the whole Assembly to its feet in roaring applause. Even one of his enemies felt obliged to admit: "Oh, what a brute! But what a talent!"

But Mirabeau was an independent thinker. Much as he wanted to see justice and equality established, he also believed France needed its king. In fact, a chief reason he supported the Constitution was that it would allow the King to wield his authority more effectively and justly.

By the fall of 1789 Mirabeau was convinced that, because of the growing hostility toward the King, France was fast descending into anarchy. For the good of his country he felt obliged to begin pulling away from the Assembly. In October 1789 he quietly began to urge the King to take steps to gain back his rightful authority.

The Assembly almost immediately began to suspect Mirabeau of treachery. But Mirabeau would not last long in the favor of the royal court either, for by now Louis strongly opposed the Constitution that Mirabeau tried to convince him would strengthen his position. After just a few months in the pay of the King, Mirabeau had to face the fact that Louis could not ever be the strong constitutional monarch he so urgently wanted for his country. "What woolgatherers they are! What bunglers! How cowardly," he remarked of the King and Queen.

In the following months Mirabeau grew increasingly unpopular with the royal court. At the same time, following the typical seesaw of public opinion, he found himself once again respected in the Assembly. In January 1791 he was elected its president. A sense of urgency possessed him now. He saw that the Revolution had gotten out of control, and he began to despair of being able to reverse its direction.

Mirabeau's tireless efforts to hold the Revolution within bounds, coupled with his wild personal habits, soon began to catch up with him. By spring the once inexhaustible Comte was confined to his bed.

On April 2, 1791, Mirabeau died. With his passing, the Revolution experienced one of its first great losses. As he had predicted, the anarchy and violence continued to increase. It has been said that the fiery and independent Mirabeau was perhaps the only one who, had he lived, might have been able to change this course of events.

It was not his good looks that inspired such deference. With bulging eyes, a head too large for his body, and a gaudy, rather tasteless style of dressing, Mirabeau was generally regarded as ugly. Nor did he command respect because of his character. Mirabeau had been involved in a number of scandals with women, shady financial deals, and other tangles with the law. His reputation for testiness and even downright rudeness was well known.

Mirabeau was genuinely interested in the welfare of his country and, in spite of his off-putting appearance and unseemly behavior, had an uncanny understanding of the ways of men, which gave him a reputation as a kind of political genius.

The Manège each day saw a full round of speeches and debates, but it was by no means the only center of political activity in Paris. With the coming of the Assembly, scores of political clubs and societies sprang up.

In December 1789 a small group of the more radical delegates gathered in the musty hall of an old Dominican monastery. Many of them had been the brains behind the all-night session of August 4; others had helped to direct the October 6 march to Versailles. Now they formed a club whose members, pledged to support state control of all authority, could meet to debate and discuss issues. Its impact was to be so great that for decades its name would be as feared and reviled as "communist" has been in our time.

The club, which came to be called the Jacobin Club after the order of the old monastery ("Jacobin" was a popular term for Dominican), soon became one of the principal centers of revolutionary activity. At first membership was limited to deputies in the Assembly, but after several months nondeputies were also allowed to join. Soon its membership numbered many hundreds, and branch clubs formed in outlying provinces.

For those who couldn't afford the Jacobin Club (which charged annual dues too steep for members of the working class) there was the Cordeliers Club. This group included in its ranks revolutionary figures such as Georges Danton, who would soon hold center stage in Paris. The large working-class element of its membership often made for raucous scenes on the debate floor.

There were numerous other clubs as well, including several for those who had more conservative leanings. The royalist Salon Français hatched numerous plots to kidnap the King or reinstate him with full powers.

A Constitution Is Drafted

In the relative calm of 1790 all this political activity yielded a rich harvest. The Declaration of the Rights of Man and the Citizen spoke of the lofty ideals of freedom and equality. By 1791 France would have a new constitution setting forth the precise means by which these ideals would be achieved.

The Constitution of 1791 established a new, basic framework for the nation's government. The power to make laws was given to a new governing body, the Legislative Assembly, whose members were to be elected every two years. The Assembly would also have the power to declare war, ratify treaties, and set taxes.

The power of the King, by contrast, was much reduced. He was required to swear an oath to be faithful to the nation and to uphold the Constitution. He had the power to veto certain legislation, but there was a provision for his veto to be overridden. The power he had once had, through special agents called *intendants*, over local affairs throughout France was now in the hands of popularly elected local officials.

Another principal way in which the new Constitution sought to safeguard liberty was by overhauling the judicial system. Under the old regime the King had had the power to throw someone into prison at whim, regardless of whether there was concrete evidence that he or she had committed a crime. And persons found guilty were often subjected to torture or to humiliating punishments. After 1790 many things changed. Judges were to be elected by the people and cases tried in various local courts. Trials were opened to the public, and the use of juries was introduced for criminal cases. The nation's penal code was also overhauled. Torture was abolished, new punishments that better fit various crimes were introduced, and the death penalty was reserved for only the most serious offenses.

And, of course, freedom of speech was expressly guaranteed. From the summer of 1789 on, nearly all censorship of books and newspapers ceased.

As important as liberty to the men of the Assembly was the ideal of equality. The delegates stopped short of granting full political equality to Frenchmen. Wary of what might happen if the poor and uneducated were allowed to vote and run for office, they made the ability to pay taxes amounting to three days' wages a requirement for voting. An even steeper income requirement was set for those who wished to run for certain important offices. (Actually, this belief that financial stability or property ownership made a man responsible enough to vote or hold office was commonplace among Enlightenment theorists; in the early years of the United States, voters also had to meet property requirements.)

Although there were a few who pressed for expanding women's rights, most delegates took it for granted that women would not be granted the same rights of citizenship as men. Nor were slaves and free blacks in the French colonies granted citizenship, despite the antislavery sentiments of many revolutionaries. In September 1791 the Assembly washed its hands of the issue by turning over to the colonies the right to regulate the political status of their black residents.

Still, the Assembly's achievement was remarkable for its time. While many artisans and poorer townspeople were barred from voting, many peasants, because they owned some land and hence paid taxes, were allowed to vote. In all, over four million Frenchmen qualified to vote. And even those who were only "passive" citizens still shared the other rights of citizenship with their voting neighbors.

The Constitution of 1791 also did much to ensure that Frenchmen would have far greater equality of opportunity than they had in the past. Under the *ancien régime* most positions in the court and the armed forces had been restricted to noblemen and those wealthy bourgeois who could afford to pay handsomely for them. Now the sale of offices was completely eliminated. The business of government would fall largely to elected officials.

In the army, members of the third estate would be eligible for all ranks, and officers' commissions would be filled chiefly from the ranks or on the basis of competitive exams. In addition, a National Guard was created to stand beside the regular army. The Guard was open to all active citizens, and its officers were elected. A prestigious career in the armed forces, once the dream of only a few, was now within grasp of many thousands of Frenchmen.

Although it was not finally approved until the fall of 1791, a number of the Constitution's reforms were put into effect before that date. The result was a growing excitement as people watched their nation's rebirth.

The Change in Governmental Administration

	ANCIEN RÉGIME	NATIONAL ASSEMBLY

THE FLOW OF POWER:

ANCIEN RÉGIME

King
↓
Royal Council
↓
intendants
↓
people

NATIONAL ASSEMBLY

King
(supervised by Assembly)
↓
ministers of central government
⇅
directors   procurator   municipal
(in districts,   corps;
departments)   mayor
(in towns)

people

CHIEF ADMINISTRATIVE OFFICIALS:	*intendant*	*municipal corps and mayor*	*directors*	*procurator*
HOW CHOSEN	selected by King	elected by townspeople	elected by people of dept. or district	elected by townspeople
UNIT PRESIDED OVER	généralité (34 total)	town	department (approximately 80 total) or district	—
AREAS OF AUTHORITY	levying taxes, conscription of militia, regulation of markets, supervision of police, administration of schools	levying taxes, conscription of militia, regulation of markets, supervision of police, administration of schools		served as link with central administration

Généralité: The basic administrative unit of the *ancien régime*, overseen by an intendent; there were 34 généralités altogether.

Intendant: An administrative official who represented the royal government within an assigned généralité, performing such functions as supervising tax collection, recruiting soldiers, and overseeing the courts.

Festival of the Fédération

The streets of Paris were packed. The windows spilled over with eager onlookers. Great cheers filled the air as spectators first caught sight of the marchers approaching the Champ de Mars. The banners of the nation's various departments (provinces) waved above their heads, bright splashes of color against the rainy gray sky. These were joined by hundreds of brilliant blue uniforms—those of the National Guard.

The first Festival of the Fédération, held July 14, 1790, expressed the sense of national pride and unity that the new government hoped to instill in Frenchmen and -women. In the years to follow, elaborate festivals such as this played an important role in expressing and shaping people's feelings about the Revolution. *Cultural Services of the French Embassy.*

The occasion was the first anniversary of the storming of the Bastille, and the people of France had gone all out to celebrate. In Paris twelve thousand workmen, assisted by local citizens, had dug up the huge public square called the Champ de Mars to create turf seats for spectators. Enthusiastic revolutionaries from every department of France had converged on Paris to take part in a procession from the Bastille to this huge, new amphitheater.

Three hundred thousand sat in the rain for hours in order to catch a glimpse of the elaborate ceremonies. Their wait was well rewarded. The celebration included a Mass said by three hundred priests wearing tricolor* stoles. Music was provided by an orchestra of twelve hundred musicians. To highlight it all, there was to be an appearance by the King and Queen.

The cannons had been fired. A hush fell over the crowd. Louis XVI rose and began to address his people. "I, King of the French, swear to employ the power delegated to me in maintaining the Constitution decreed by the National Assembly and accepted by me." Immediately hundreds of cries of "Long live the King!" broke the silence, with accents of every region of the nation melting together into one great cheer.

The ceremony had grown out of a new spirit of national pride and brotherhood that had been spreading across the country. It had been the work of hundreds of men who called themselves *fédérés*, men whose goal was for Frenchmen and -women of all provinces to lay aside regional differences and "to be free together." As the festivities of July 14 drew to a close, it seemed their dream had become a reality.

Underneath the sentiments of unity and harmony in which the nation was caught up, however, new seeds of strife and discord had begun to sprout.

The three colors blue, white, and red had become the revolutionaries' symbol of national unity. Red and blue were the colors of Paris, and white the color of the King's family.

Reforms and the Church

Far from being atheists, freethinkers, or deists, most of the delegates to the National Assembly were sincere Christians. They had promised to found the new government on "the sacred basis of religion"—and they meant it. In fact, most were not only Christian but Catholic. Enough of them maintained the old French suspicion of Protestants (who had been forbidden officially to worship openly under the regime of Louis XVI) that the Declaration of Rights made only a timid reference to the religious freedom it in fact granted. However, years of abuses by the Church, fanned by the anticlerical literature of the Enlightenment, had given the delegates' faith a skeptical, hard-nosed quality. Many shared the suspicion of the Church's great wealth and privilege that writers such as Voltaire had voiced.

It was not surprising, then, that many delegates voted for legislation that would strip the Church of its old power and wealth. The issue that brought old resentments toward the Church to the fore was simple: money. Although the delegates had done a masterful job of reorganizing the nation's administration, France's financial situation was still poor.

The Assembly was reluctant to levy new taxes, for fear of alienating the bourgeois property owners who were the backbone of the Revolution. Instead the proposal was made to take over, or nationalize, property that belonged to the Church. The vast tracts of Church land then could be sold, and bank notes based on these sales could be issued.

The vote was close, with such well-known clergy as the Abbé Sieyès defending the Church and accusing the delegates of "bourgeois envy," "private vengeances," and "animosity toward the clergy." Nevertheless, on November 2, 1789, the Assembly passed the motion. The next month Church lands went on the auction block. The bank notes that were issued, called *assignats*, were soon to become a form of common currency.

Once the process of intervening in the affairs of the Church had begun, it was natural that intervention should spread to other areas. The Assembly proposed several bold and sweeping changes.

The first reform measures concerned the nation's monasteries and convents. For years writers had poked fun at the decadence of monks and nuns, painting scathing portraits of the rich men and women who led genteel, sheltered lives in buildings that looked more like châteaux than homes for those who had taken vows of poverty. The first reform the Assembly passed was a call for the abolition of monastic orders. Monks and nuns presently in monasteries or convents would be given a choice of either leaving and accepting state pensions or of continuing under their vows in convents or monasteries to be designated by the state. No new monastic vows would be permitted.

Next the Assembly turned its attention to the regular clergy. A committee on the Church came up with a plan to treat priests and bishops as any other public officials. Their salaries would be paid by the state, and all excessively high and low salaries would be adjusted. Bishops would be elected just like other officials.

The deputies saw nothing out of line with their plans, which became known as the Civil Constitution of the Clergy. There was precedent for the state to set Church policy; for example, French kings before Louis XVI had suppressed monastic orders. Many of the clergy saw little in the plans with which they would quarrel. There was widespread agreement that much about the Church was badly in need of reform. Also, the deputies had no intention of tampering with the Church's beliefs or ceremonies.

On July 12, just two days before the grand celebration of the *fédérés* was to take place, the Assembly passed the Civil Constitution of the Clergy. Ten days later the King gave the measure his provisional sanction. All that was needed now was the approval of the Pope.

But there was the rub. One of the chief tenets of Roman Catholicism is that the Pope is the Church's supreme authority. French Catholics had chafed under that authority in the past, and there had been attempts to make the French Church more independent of Rome. But the kind of independence many of the delegates envisioned for the Church in France was of an entirely new order. Its purpose was not to make the French Church an independent spiritual voice in its own right. Instead, the delegates shared a typical Enlightenment view of the Church—that it should be the servant of the state, a sort of moral agent whose job was to make people into better citizens.

The delegates, perhaps unaware of the extent to which the philosophes had inspired them to question traditional Catholicism, were confident that the Pope's approval would be forthcoming. Some even felt it unnecessary to seek it at all. Many of the clergy were of a similar mind.

Many others, however, were not. They might go along with some of the precepts of the Revolution, but they drew the line at giving up the Church's independent spiritual authority. And Pope Pius VI, far from sharing the new view of Church-state relations, was suspicious of anything proposed by the revolutionary Assembly.

After some delay, the Pope replied that he could not approve the Constitution in its present form. Negotiations were begun immediately to reach a compromise.

Once word got out that the Pope had not approved the Assembly's plan, bishops and priests across France began to refuse to go along with it. In some areas protesters resorted to violence.

In an attempt to control the situation, the government in November 1790 passed a decree requiring all clergy to take an oath promising to be loyal to the Constitution—which included the Civil Constitution of the Clergy.

Sunday, January 2, the bells for morning Mass tolled as usual. But this was no ordinary Sunday. Men and women who hadn't been to Mass in years turned out. In addition to the overflowing congregations, the churches swelled with army officers in splendid tricolor uniforms and bands playing triumphant tunes. Parishioners cheered and booed as their clerical leaders approached government officials. The occasion was the "swearing in" of the nation's clergy. In churches all across the country, this was the date set for priests and bishops to take an oath swearing to uphold the revolutionary Constitution.

The requirement of the oath, however, only made matters worse. More than half the nation's priests refused to take the oath. Thousands of the nation's faithful, loyal to the men who had married them, baptized their children, and buried their dead, followed these priests' lead and protested the reforms. The matter was clinched in the spring, when Pope Pius VI made his condemnation of the Civil Constitution official. Hundreds of priests who had originally taken the oath retracted it. The Assembly's attempt to create a national church had failed. And less than a year after the remarkable display of national unity shown at the celebration of the *fédérés*, France was fast on its way to becoming a nation divided.

3

Chronology

1789–1791

émigrés leave

•

1790

growth of political clubs, such as the Jacobins
and Cordeliers

•

1791

winter and spring	growing alienation of the King, provoked by Civil Constitution of the Clergy and its condemnation by the Pope
June 20	King's flight to Varennes sans-culottes grow angry
July 17	Champ de Mars Massacre
September 14	new Constitution accepted by King
October 1	Legislative Assembly meets
fall	rise of Girondins

•

1792

April 20	war declared on Austria
spring	dissatisfaction grows among sans-culottes
June 20	invasion of Tuileries
July 11	decree of *"La Patrie en Danger!"*
July	*fédérés* arrive in Paris from provinces
August 10	King is overthrown Commune formed in Paris

Chapter Three:
Spreading Conflict

Just two days after the fall of the Bastille, a coach pulled out of the elegant gates of Versailles. Inside could be seen the masses of curls sported by the King's playboy brother, the Comte d'Artois. The Count was outraged by what he saw as the King's cowardly refusal to defend the nation's nobility and their way of life. He, for one, would not accept being ruled by a bunch of rowdy and headstrong commoners.

The Counterrevolution

Artois and his family were the first of thousands of French noblemen to leave the country. During the two weeks after their departure a steady stream of carriages loaded with trunks and packages left Versailles and headed for the border. By the end of July many of the King's principal courtiers had gone. Following the rioting and pillaging of the Great Fear, many more took flight. And after the march on Versailles, yet another wave of nobles headed for foreign soil. It was not long before France was ringed by small communities of émigrés.

At first the emigration of the aristocracy was largely a gesture of protest. "We shall return in three months," the Comte d'Artois had remarked on leaving. But as the Revolution progressed and it became clear that the old order of life was fast being swept away, some of the émigrés saw a need to take action beyond merely leaving. The Comte d'Artois and another leading courtier, the Prince of Conde, began to organize these émigré communities into a formidable counterrevolutionary force.

The outbreak of the Revolution had fanned the peasants' old fears of aristocratic plots and foreign invasions. These fears turned out to be justified. By 1791 the émigrés had already tried twice, unsuccessfully, to rescue the King. They had secretly schemed to foment riots in the south of France. And they had begun negotiations with foreign rulers to enlist their help for an invasion of France.

Many Europeans had been sympathetic to the Revolution at first. The liberal nobility saw it as a praiseworthy attack on despotic rule. In England and Germany in particular, where the ideas of the Enlightenment had made the deepest inroads, there was a great swell of enthusiasm. For over a decade many in England had been pressing for various kinds of governmental reform that would give the common people a greater voice in Parliament. After several defeats, events in France renewed their hope of change. But the widespread rioting and château burning that followed the fall of the Bastille soon began to turn the tide of international opinion.

"The deepest, the most craftily devised, the best combined and the most extensive design that ever was carried on, since the beginning of the world, against all property, all order, all religion, all law, and all real freedom"—this was how English philosopher Edmund Burke characterized the French Revolution. Burke's eloquent attack on the Revolution, *Reflections on the French Revolution,* struck a resounding chord with his fellow Englishmen, leery both of the British reform movement and of the revolt in France. For nearly two decades afterward the British Parliament passed few reforms of any kind. *Reflections,* which was a condemnation of basic natural rights philosophy as well as of the French Revolution, found eager readers among the ruling elites all over the European continent. Antirevolutionary sentiment was spreading.

When the smooth-talking Comte d'Artois appealed to the monarchs of Europe for aid in an attack on the new revolutionary government, he had every reason to expect that they would rush to support his cause. Most of them, however, were hesitant. In part this was because the revolutionary government still seemed too weak to be a real threat. But in large measure it was because Louis himself was not cooperating with the counterrevolutionaries.

Until the passage of the Civil Constitution of the Clergy, the King stood apart from the plots and protestations of his brother and the other émigrés. He suspected, with some reason, that if the émigrés were successful in their plots to rescue him, he would be forever indebted to the aristocracy. Louis and Marie Antoinette were as reluctant to see themselves as puppets of a powerful nobility as to wind up controlled by the reigning bourgeoisie. Also, Louis still harbored the hope that he might somehow reverse the recent course of events and regain his lost authority.

However, the Civil Constitution of the Clergy, in particular the requirement of an oath of loyalty from all clergy, changed all that. For Louis, who was by nature a pious and religiously conservative man, it was the last straw. He had a strong loyalty to his Church and to the Pope who headed it, and he was deeply troubled by the new laws. He listened in horror to tales of convents being broken into, church doors being covered with graffiti, and effigies, or likenesses, of the Pope being burned. Now when his brother Artois and others spoke to him of plans for escape or for foreign invasion, Louis listened.

The Flight to Varennes

It was dark as Marie Antoinette dressed her son and daughter. The young girl stared at her brother as the Queen slipped a girl's dress over his head. "What do you think we are going to do?" she asked in a whisper. "I suppose to act in a play, since we have got these funny clothes on," the young prince replied sleepily. But it was not a time to talk. Their mother hushed the two children and walked them quietly through empty rooms to a coach waiting in the dark.

An hour later, a gentleman clad in a dark-green overcoat and gray wig made his way to the palace exit. For the last twelve nights the gray-wigged Chevalier de Coigny, known to look much like the King, had marched by at just this hour. The sentry standing guard nodded with familiarity as the gentleman passed. Only tonight, shortly after he had passed the sentry, the man in the overcoat headed for the carriage into which the two children had climbed not long before. "Papa!" the princess cried softly as he entered. By midnight, unknown to all but a handful, the King and Queen and their two children had left the palace.

Outside the gates of the city, in the darkness before sunrise, the royal family transferred into a larger dark-green carriage with plush, white velvet upholstery that had recently become a regular sight along the road east. They traveled steadily throughout the night. When the sun came up and there was no sign that anyone was following them, the King sighed with relief. Yet he could not really breathe easily until they had reached the villages near the eastern border, where counterrevolutionary troops had promised to meet them.

The carriage was luxurious, but so large and heavily laden that even with six horses it could go no faster than seven miles an hour. Before long it was hours behind the planned schedule. In the eastern villages where counterrevolutionary troops were stationed, local peasants grew suspicious of the crowds of mounted soldiers that had been milling around for hours. Many thought they were there to collect overdue rents. In Sainte Menehould the captain gave his men permission to go into the local tavern and have a drink to relieve some of the tension.

So when the elegant, dark-green carriage pulled up at the post house in Sainte Menehould and ordered a change of horses, there were no troops to be seen. A look of concern spread across the passengers' faces.

Although the soldiers had left the scene, the villagers, still suspicious, had not. And the villagers' suspicions were not easily banished.

Dozens of pairs of eyes followed the carriage's every movement. They watched intently as the commander of the strange soldiers rode up, saluted its occupants, quickly whispered something to the man inside, and galloped off. One of the onlookers was the village postmaster, Jean-Baptiste Drouet. While in the army the young Drouet had seen the Queen at least once, and was struck by the resemblance the woman in the carriage bore to her. But he could not be absolutely sure and did not want to get into trouble.

Meanwhile, back in Paris the alarm bells were ringing and crowds were massing around the Tuileries palace. That morning the King's valet had pulled back the bed curtains promptly at seven o'clock, only to find the bed empty. Before long, General Lafayette had issued an order for the capture of the royal family and their return to Paris, and riders had galloped off in all directions to search for the escaped King and Queen.

Late that afternoon Drouet received word from one of the riders who had stopped at a nearby village that the King had escaped. The young postmaster's suspicions were confirmed. In no time, he and a friend were galloping furiously off on the road to the border.

About midnight the green carriage lumbered into the small village of Varennes. "Halt! One step more and we fire," a voice boomed. The passengers, who claimed to be the Baroness von Kroff and her steward and children, were ushered into a small room above the store of the village procurator. But a local judge who had lived for several years at Versailles had been sent for. The strangers' claims would soon be put to the test. Before the days of photographs, the *personal* identification of suspects was critical. As he entered the door to the small room, the judge stopped abruptly and dropped to his knees. There was no question. This supposed steward was indeed his King. The game was up.

By seven thirty the next morning, Louis and Marie Antoinette and their two children had climbed, bleary-eyed, back into the carriage. Surrounded by National Guardsmen, the party began the long, hot

This engraving shows the apprehension of Louis XVI at Varennes, after his attempted escape. *Culver Pictures, Inc.*

journey back to Paris. All along the way crowds taunted them, often beating on the carriage windows. They yelled out insults so violent that the young prince was brought to tears. For much of the trip Louis was silent. But at one point he remarked dejectedly, "There is no longer a King in France."

There was good reason for his dejection. The King would now face a people who knew he had been scheming behind their backs to join with counterrevolutionary forces.

Even in the face of this blatant act of betrayal, most of the leaders of the National Assembly were still reluctant to let go of their hopes for a constitutional monarchy. The Assembly had suspended the King from his royal functions and begun to pass legislation without waiting for royal approval. Yet they still did not want to remove Louis from the throne and leave France without a king. Some hoped that his recent humiliation would make him willing at last to grant the compromises they sought. Others feared that dethronement would threaten foreign rulers and bring on foreign attack. And many of the Assembly leaders, bourgeois men with homes and property, were concerned that taking such a step might bring the working classes to power. Starting with the storming of the Bastille, events had led them to associate the nation's working class with violence, destruction, and general anarchy.

The Rise of the Sans-Culottes

Indeed, the Assembly had cause to worry about the workers in the cities. Before the flight to Varennes, Louis had still enjoyed a surprising degree of popularity among the people. For generations the French had been raised to love and revere their monarch, and such traditions die hard. In the aftermath of the storming of the Bastille, all Louis had to do was accept the tricolor cockade, the new emblem of the Revolution, for the people's eyes to tear and the great hall of the Hôtel de Ville to fill with cries of "Our King! Our father!" and "Long live the King!"

But the news of the King's flight dashed much of whatever popularity the King still commanded. The popular press was full of cartoons portraying the royal family as pigs. In some of the provinces the aftermath of the King's flight brought on a new wave of château burnings. Several of the provincial Jacobin clubs called for the dethronement of the King. They also began to call for the creation of a new, more radically democratic government: a *republic*, a government in which a king would play no part and in which the "people," meaning all men, not just the wealthy, would have a say.

At the start of the Revolution, the third estate had presented a united front. Peasants and working people readily accepted the leadership of the bourgeoisie. But since 1790 a number of working people known as *sans-culottes* (meaning "without knee breeches," a name they earned because they did not wear the tight, knee-length breeches of the aristocracy but long workmen's trousers instead) had been developing a political consciousness all their own. The political involvement of these people grew to such a degree that eventually the term "sans-culotte" was used to describe any politically active citizen. The flight to Varennes merely speeded up their growing political activity.

Workingmen often tended to look for simple, bold, and direct solutions. It seemed to them that most of the bourgeois Assembly delegates did not have their interests much at heart. They had little patience for complex schemes to wheedle small concessions out of a reluctant King. Denied a significant role in the Assembly and other new political bodies by the property qualifications for voting and holding office, they sought other forums.

Setting the Scene:
Trousers and Other Revolutionary Fashions

In 1770 local governments in France were run by men in close-fitted green-and-purple satin coats with silver buttons, velvet waistcoats elaborately embroidered in colored silk and gold thread, and large pieces of lace (called jabots) spilling from their neckpieces. Pristine white stockings and skintight satin pants that stopped at the knees adorned their legs.

Twenty years later many of the men setting local policy presented a very different picture. Instead of brightly colored satins, silks, and velvets, their clothes were of plain wool, usually in black or brown or other simple colors. Their coats and waistcoats were loose and unadorned. They wore no lace at the throat, no gold or silver buttons, and—perhaps most noticeably—full-length trousers instead of knee breeches.

This last innovation earned the radical republicans of the French Revolution the scornful nickname of "sans-culottes."

Why were the members of an important political faction known by the clothes they wore? Throughout the Revolution, politics and fashions were linked. The decision of some men with republican views to wear trousers, for example, was largely political. And from 1789 to 1795 the rapid and dramatic changes in French costume matched the tumultuous course political events took in those years.

With the rise to power of the bourgeoisie, all forms of dress associated with the aristocracy quickly disappeared. To be seen sporting the elaborate, showy fabrics, styles, and jewelry of the *ancien régime* could actually prove dangerous. In their place a whole new way of dressing emerged. Men, even those who had not adopted the radical views or pant style of the sans-culottes,

Styles were much simplified over the course of the Revolution. The dress of the woman second from the left, with its high waist and body-skimming silhouette, shows the influence of ancient Greece. *Art Resource/Lauros-Giraudon.*

still abandoned the silks, satins, brocades, and embroidery of earlier years. Instead, they took their cue from the black suits that were the required dress of delegates of the third estate and confined their clothes to dark, plain, somber materials. In fact, the French Revolution marked the end of centuries of masculine finery and the beginning of the era of conservative menswear that has continued until very nearly the present day.

Women's styles underwent an equally dramatic transformation. Like men, well-to-do women of the *ancien régime* were accustomed to dressing in clothes that drew attention to their wealth and to the fact that they did no manual work. Their high, powdered hairstyles required hours to create, and their wide skirts made any movement an ordeal.

In searching for new styles to replace these, the revolutionaries turned for inspiration to the clothes of ancient Greece, which many considered to be the birthplace of true democracy. By 1795 high-waisted "slip-dresses" made of plain, thin muslin were the rage. These Grecian-style gowns required none of the elaborate corsetting of the older styles and were worn absolutely plain, with no ornament at all. The style was short-lived due to its impracticality in northern climates (the sheer muslin provided almost no protection from cold or damp). Still, throughout the revolutionary period women's styles remained simple, flowing, and natural, and largely free from adornment. And some vestiges of the Greek style proved enduring. These included the natural hairstyle of curls drawn onto the forehead and the taste for high waists, both of which lasted into the 1800s.

When the French Revolution ended in 1795, men and women returned to some of the fashion habits of prerevolutionary days. They once again wore jewels and silks. But the years 1789 to 1795 had altered the way people dressed as much as they had the way they were governed.

Every day saw scores of carpenters, shopkeepers, newspaper hawkers, young apprentices, and other workingmen milling around the entrance to a modest building on the Rue Dauphine. On warm days the sound of heated and urgent voices wafted into the air through the open windows. Here was the Cordeliers Club, the political club opened in April 1790 to provide a forum for those poorer citizens who could not meet the stiff entrance requirements of the more selective Jacobin Club. Dues at the Cordeliers Club were only two *sous* a month.

The Club's location was a fortunate one. It was situated in the section of Paris where dozens of journalists, printers, and book dealers made their homes. Its cafés were frequented by such well-known, radical writers and lawyers as Camille Desmoulins, the passionate, sallow-faced young lawyer who had first stirred the people to move on the Bastille. Almost overnight the Club and its members became principal spokesmen for radical, antimonarchical views. They were a politically powerful force.

Setting the Scene:
The Jacobins

In 1781 a businessman planning the wedding of his daughter would most likely contact the local curé to make arrangements. In 1791 he might well reserve the local Jacobin hall. In 1781 a working-class family, down on its luck, might be brought a basket of food and clothing by the nuns at the local convent. In 1791 such a family might receive a similar basket from the local Jacobins.

In June 1789 a group of delegates to the Estates General from Brittany began to meet before sessions at a local coffeehouse to decide which way they would vote and to support one another in sticking to their convictions. Within twelve months the group, whose name had changed from the Breton Club to the Society of Friends of the Constitution, and then to the Jacobins (after the order of monks who had occupied their first official home), had expanded to include affiliated clubs all over France. Its meetings, activities, and clubhouses had become as dominant a force in the lives of many French citizens as the Church had been just a few years earlier.

The first function of the Jacobin clubs was political activity. Members used just about any tactic they thought would help ensure that votes in the Assembly were in accord with republican principles and virtues—freedom, equality, and representative and constitutional government.

This contemporary drawing satirizes a meeting of the Jacobin Club of Paris. The occasion was the hotly debated decision of the spring of 1792 to declare war on France's enemies. *The Bettmann Archive.*

One of the main ways in which members sought to influence public opinion was through the printed word. The clubs—primarily the mother club in Paris—churned out thousands of pamphlets and circulars, and even several newspapers. In some clubs over half the money taken in went toward printing costs. Printed materials were then distributed to other clubs throughout the nation. Most clubs opened reading rooms in which these pamphlets, circulars, and a long list of revolutionary newspapers were made available to readers.

In addition to producing propaganda, Jacobins spent a great deal of time petitioning and electioneering. They drew up lists of candidates, canvassed votes for them, and managed to seat Jacobins on all manner of local governing bodies. In some towns as many as one third or even one half of the members of the local Jacobin club served in some elected office. Jacobins also petitioned both the national government and local governments on dozens of concerns, down to when army officers should be forced to begin wearing the new national uniform or whether a particular town's post office should be moved.

As the Revolution progressed and the Jacobins moved from being a minority to the "party" in power, the activities of the clubs changed. No longer exclusively political, they expanded to become the central spiritual, educational, and moral force in their members' lives. More and more, meetings came to resemble church services. Most included the singing of revolutionary "hymns" and moral talks very like sermons that were delivered before a blue-white-and-red "altar of the nation." Weddings and christenings were held in clubhouses, and children were encouraged to attend "Sunday schools" where they learned to memorize the Declaration of the Rights of Man and the Citizen. Processions in which busts of revolutionary heroes or young girls dressed as goddesses of reason were paraded through the town took the place of the religious processions of old.

Jacobin clubs also took over much of the charitable work that had formerly fallen to the Church. In Toulouse the local club's committee of good works distributed bread to dozens of needy people, and provided furniture for a soldier's widow and support for an orphan. In addition, clubs tended to affairs as diverse as rewarding citizens for heroic deeds, seeing that towns removed dung in order to improve public sanitation, and even tracing lost packages.

At the height of power, the Jacobins' numbers included approximately one out of every twelve Frenchmen, who together formed over six thousand chapters. Yet even these figures only hint at their influence.

Parisian workers and others who favored more radical changes found another forum in the local governments that had been established in each section of the city. These sectional governments, of which there were forty-eight, had become the scenes of rousing speeches that called for direct democracy and frequently chided the Assembly for its timidity and conservatism.

Ever since the return of the King to Paris, the section assemblies and the Cordeliers Club had called loudly for the creation of a republic. But when the Assembly met to debate what action to take, the gap between the sans-culottes and the bourgeois delegates was clearly evident. On July 15, 1791, the delegates voted to find Louis innocent of all guilt in the flight to Varennes and to restore him to his office, if he accepted the revised Constitution.

The Champ de Mars Massacre

Immediately after the vote there was heated talk among the Cordeliers about how to respond. By Saturday July 16, a plan was well under way. Petitions calling for the trial of the King and a new republican government were drafted, and these, bearing thousands of signatures, were presented to the delegates of the Assembly. The petitions were

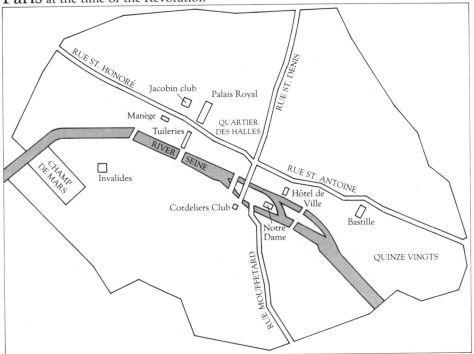

drawn up hastily right in the great open square of the Champ de Mars and immediately placed on the Altar of the Fatherland, which had been erected for the celebration, held two days earlier, of the second anniversary of the fall of the Bastille. By the afternoon of Sunday the 17th, hundreds of people had massed around the altar, each stepping up in turn to add his or her name—or, in a number of cases, the "X" of the illiterate—to the document.

Suddenly, two men were spotted under the steps leading up to the Altar. Were they there to look up the women's skirts? some wondered. Then the cry went up: "Spies! Spies of the counterrevolution!" And with that, the crowd was transformed in a matter of seconds into a lynch mob. The two "peeping Toms" were seized and taken out and hanged on the spot.

It did not take long for reports of the incident to reach the city officials and the National Guard. Within hours Mayor Bailly declared martial law, and Lafayette set out with a contingent of the National Guard for the Champ de Mars.

The guardsmen were greeted by boos and the hurling of stones. Lafayette ordered the rioters to disperse. Yet the stones kept coming. Then, piercing the hubbub of the name-callers, came the deadly command: "Fire!"

When the volley was over, fifty of the demonstrators lay dead or close to death.

The Revolutionaries Divided

The Champ de Mars Massacre, as it came to be called, ended once and for all the notion that the Revolution was a single, united movement. Now there were clearly two main camps: the moderates, who wanted to make peace with the King and put an end to disorder, and those who favored dethroning the King and creating a republic. Many of those in the second group were working people who stood ready to use violence, if needed, to achieve their ends. Each group believed the other, as much as the aristocracy, was the enemy of the nation.

For the time being the moderates had the upper hand. After the Champ de Mars incident, martial law was kept in force, the presses of the sans-culotte newspapers were seized, the Cordeliers Club was closed, and orders were put out for the arrest of radical leaders like Desmoulins. Even the Jacobin Club, at one time a chief home to radical politicians, came close to folding. The vast majority of its members left to form a new club of more moderate views—the Feuillants.

By September a final, revised draft of the Constitution was presented to the nation. The revised version still set forth a plan for a constitutional monarchy, and, as the moderates had hoped, the King was willing to sign it.

To many it seemed the Revolution was over. The Assembly had done what it had set out to do. The King, now that he had agreed to abide by the Constitution, had been restored to power. The strife and divisiveness of the summer, it appeared, were things of the past. Paris went all out to celebrate. The King was carried aloft in a triumphant ceremony, and all over the city there were toasts, dances, and gay processions.

But the peace of the fall was an uneasy one at best. Just below the surface, old tensions and bitterness were still unresolved. The radicals had been silenced by the repressive measures of the late summer. But they had not forgotten the Champ de Mars incident.

The Rise of the Girondins

The autumn saw the rise to power of a new group of radicals. The acceptance of the new Constitution meant that a whole new legislature, the Legislative Assembly, had to be elected. (The National Assembly, which it would replace, was to be dissolved now that its work of producing a constitution was complete.) Most of the delegates elected to the new Legislative Assembly were moderates—over one third of them joined the Feuillant Club. But a group of especially talented men of strong republican views soon made their presence felt. They brought new life to the Jacobin Club, and their influence in the new assembly was out of all proportion to their numbers.

These delegates came to be known as Girondins, because many of them were from the part of France on the southern Atlantic coast known as the Gironde. They were, relatively, young—ranging in age from twenty-six to thirty-eight—and their views were radical. Many of them had a talent for public speaking and had made a name for themselves in provincial Jacobin circles. Now they were eager to make their mark on Paris. They took as their leader Jacques Pierre Brissot, the ambitious publisher of one of Paris' revolutionary papers. Their social life centered around the salon of Madame Manon Roland, the brilliant and idealistic wife of an older civil servant. Madame Roland had a solid grounding in the classics and a thorough knowledge of Rousseau and the other philosophes. Indeed, she had developed a positive passion for the ideas of Rousseau. The Girondins were attracted by her idealism and intelligence.

Within weeks of taking office the Girondins were actively pressing for measures against the groups they considered to be enemies of the Revolution. They wanted the émigrés ordered to return to France under threat of death. And they wanted members of the clergy who had refused to take the oath to uphold the Civil Constitution of the Clergy to be ordered to leave the country. By the end of November, they had persuaded the Assembly to pass both measures.

Many of the Girondins were also very progressive when it came to the plight of the blacks in France's colonies; Brissot was the head of the "Friends of the Blacks," the nation's antislavery society. By spring they passed legislation granting equal rights to all free blacks and mulattoes.

Characters in the Revolutionary Drama: *Madame Roland*

It was an afternoon like any other in the modest second-floor apartment in the Hôtel Britannique. The day's Assembly meeting had recently closed, and one by one young men in somber dark suits began to fill the room's numerous chairs.

The scene seemed more typical of a British men's club than of Paris society. In France men and women had mingled on a nearly equal basis for some time. Yet here there was but one woman present. Dressed simply in a striped gown and a modest white shawl over her shoulders, she sat behind the men, her head bent over embroidery. She remained silent throughout the meeting, except to inquire about her guests' comfort. Neither her duties as a hostess nor her needlework were the primary focus of the woman's attention, however. A careful observer might have caught her biting her lip to squelch a few words of judgment after several of the speakers finished.

This was the influential revolutionary salon of Madame Manon Roland. These sober, high-minded meetings at Madame Roland's apartment were a far cry from the *ancien régime*'s fashionable salons with their gossip and idle chatter. They instead bore the stamp of a new breed of woman—a woman of the Revolution.

Manon Roland was in many respects the model woman of the new age. The daughter of a Paris engraver, Gatien Phlipon, she was born into the artisan class—one of the "common people." From early on Manon displayed a passionate and idealistic nature. Girls received little formal education in those days, but Manon's family kept her plentifully supplied with books. By the age of twenty she had devoured most of the great philosophers' works, and many of those by the more contemporary philosophes as well.

At the age of twenty-two Manon discovered Jean-Jacques Rousseau. This was the writer who was, at last, to give her the cause to live for that she had been seeking. In fact, Manon Phlipon's life was so profoundly influenced and shaped by Rousseau that it can be seen as an example of the great writer's ideas in action.

Manon identified with Rousseau's championing of the common people. For the rest of her life, in her dress and in the furnishing of her home, she would exhibit his contempt for upper-class luxuries. And her readiness to work for the good of her fellow countrymen and countrywomen would eventually make this reclusive young woman one of the great political figures of the age.

Manon Phlipon was as moved by Rousseau's ideas on love, marriage, and woman's place as she was by his political and moral philosophy. In his immensely popular novels Rousseau painted a glowing picture of womanly fulfillment that consisted in devoting oneself to the happiness of one's husband and children.

This became Mademoiselle Phlipon's goal as she made her way through her courting years.

Manon married a man much older and more experienced than herself, a plain-spoken civil servant and scholar of almost Puritanical uprightness named Jean-Marie Roland. For the next ten years she devoted herself to him. When she bore him a daughter, Manon poured her energies into child rearing. For the time being, her political interests seemed to have waned.

But that all changed with the events of 1789. Within days of the fall of the Bastille, Manon's letters to her friends in Paris took on a whole new tone. Charming descriptions of provincial life or anecdotes about her daughter's doings were replaced by new and passionate language. "Let France awaken and come to life! . . . Long live the people and death to the tyrants!" she ended one letter. It was not long before the Roland apartment had become the regular meeting place of a group of radical delegates known as the Girondins.

Manon Roland's Rousseauistic image of proper womanly conduct prevented her from being as active in working for her new cause as she might have liked. She always forced herself to sit in the background while meetings were being held in her home and remained silent until they were over. But she would speak her mind afterward. She also began to write anonymously for the radical press.

From the start, Madame Roland was sharply critical of her fellow revolutionaries. She expected all to share her Rousseauistic faith in a pure republic and was impatient with people whose beliefs were at all sympathetic to a constitutional monarchy or who in other ways fell short of her lofty standard.

But as the Revolution progressed, her criticisms developed a new focus. Manon Roland was committed to the goals of the Revolution, but she would not have them achieved at *any* price. After the creation of the Commune and the massacres that followed the next month, Madame Roland began to seriously question her long-standing support of the common folk. How could she support men and women who seemed actually to plot violence? Madame Roland and her fellow Girondins were caught between their belief in a republic and their dislike of the means that were being used to create it.

It was not long after the takeover of Paris by the Commune, in August 1792, that the comfortable days of the Roland salon came to an end. Radical journalists seemed to delight in hurling insults at Madame Roland. "A bordello," her salon was called.

In the middle of the night of June 2, 1793, Manon Roland was wakened by her maid. There were some "gentlemen" to see her, the distraught young woman informed her mistress. Madame Roland dressed and went to greet her guests. "We came, Citizeness, to take you into custody," they informed her.

The next five months were passed in a small dank cell. There Madame Roland maintained her dignity and quickly earned the respect of her fellow inmates. One who shared her fate commented that she had only to enter the courtyard for the other women, even coarse streetwalkers, to drop all disorderly and unmannerly conduct.

Madame Roland kept her composure right up to the end. On the day of her execution, she shared her lunch with the terrified man who was scheduled to go to the guillotine before her. Her last words—"O Liberty! what crimes are committed in thy name!"—were the final cry of a noble soul.

Movement Toward War

Louis, as might be expected, vetoed the Assembly's decrees regarding the émigrés and the dissenting clergy. At that point the Girondins and their supporters began to press for more drastic action. "Peace will set us back. . . . We can be regenerated through blood alone," wrote Madame Roland.

For some months many radicals had shared the belief that a war should be declared on the foreign powers surrounding France. They were outraged at the rulers who had allowed the émigrés to use their land as a base from which to strike out at the Revolution and were convinced that it was only a matter of time before these rulers launched an attack on revolutionary France. The Girondins were eager to strike first, before their country could be invaded. Some also had grand dreams of liberating the oppressed people in neighboring lands.

This time the King and most radicals were of a like mind about where France's interests lay. "Everything has been overturned by force and force alone can repair the damage," Marie Antoinette wrote her brother, the Emperor Leopold of the Austrian Empire. The Queen's words seemed to echo those of Madame Roland. Surprisingly, the King and Queen also wanted a war with the foreign powers—but for very different reasons.

The Girondins looked to war as a chance for the revolutionary forces to make a show of strength that would gain them bargaining power with the King. The royal family, however, expected quite opposite results. They assumed the revolutionary army would be easily beaten, thus enabling the invaders to restore the King to his former position.

There were a few who were opposed to war. Some of the most radical Jacobins, including the up-and-coming leader Maximilien Robespierre, were suspicious of any policy supported by the Queen. They were convinced that a war would be used to trick the revolutionaries in some way. But as the weeks wore on and spring approached, the voices of dissent were drowned out by the growing clamor for war.

On April 20 Louis went before the Assembly. "All would rather have war than see the dignity of the French people insulted any longer," he declared to the gathered deputies. ". . . I have now come to propose war to the National Assembly*." His address met with a

---

*Even though the Assembly's name was officially "Legislative Assembly," people still sometimes referred to it as the "National Assembly."

roar of applause. And soon he had issued the fateful declaration: War was declared on the Emperor of Austria. Within days Prussia had come to Austria's aid, and France was at war with both nations.

The outbreak of war marked a fateful turning point in the course of the Revolution. The beginning of armed combat with foreign troops ushered in a spirit of violence and division all around. Keeping pace with the battles with invading troops were increasingly violent clashes between the various revolutionary groups.

From the beginning the war proved a disaster for the French. The nation's army was not at all prepared for the undertaking to which it had just been committed. More than half of its nine thousand officers had left to join the émigrés, and many of those who remained were suspected by their men of being counterrevolutionaries. The regular troops had also been shrunk greatly by desertions. To fill the vacuum, many new volunteers had been recruited. But these men were untrained and were carried away by the new spirit of democracy in the army, which allowed them to elect their officers. All this made for a lack of discipline that soon reached the crisis stage.

When the army first clashed with the foreigners, many of the French troops panicked and fled in retreat. Others deserted to the enemy. The revolutionary forces suffered a humiliating and demoralizing defeat.

This first defeat meant the nation's peasants and working people now occupied a critical position. The only way to make up for the army's lack of discipline and leadership was with sheer numbers. And to find the hundreds of new volunteers needed, the government would have to appeal to the sans-culottes.

Dissatisfaction among the Sans-Culottes

The months before the war had been a time of great hardship for the nation's peasants and working people. The harvest of 1791 had been disastrous. The nation was plagued by runaway inflation. Fears of counterrevolutionary plots spread through the countryside. And it seemed to most people that the Assembly had no intention of taking action about these problems. "We'll soon cut the neck of the National Assembly, because it doesn't do anything," remarked one angry citizen. In Paris and throughout the provinces people had begun to take matters into their own hands, and riots had been widespread for months. The sans-culottes were particularly concerned about their precarious economic situation and pressed for a ceiling on prices. In the capital angry women had demonstrated in the markets to force grocers to fix the price of sugar.

In the region known as the Gard, twenty-five châteaux were set afire. In Etampes an angry mob, rioting for the fixing of prices, killed the mayor, whom they suspected of hoarding food. And across the nation the disastrous course the war was taking merely strengthened the people's conviction that they were being besieged by the forces of counterrevolution.

In an effort to win back support among the nation's peasants and working people, the Assembly passed several laws designed to attack the forces of counterrevolution. They set out stiff punishments for priests who refused to support the Constitution, abolished the King's personal guard, and called for an army of twenty thousand National Guardsmen to be stationed outside Paris to defend it against enemies within and without. But the first and third of these were vetoed by the King, leaving the state of affairs practically unchanged. And the Girondins still staunchly refused to take any action to fix prices.

To the leaders of the Paris sans-culottes, it was clearly time for independent action.

The Invasion of the Tuileries

The morning of June 20 the delegates of the Assembly began the day's session as usual. Suddenly shouts and cries were heard down the street, and the noise rapidly swelled and grew closer. The deputies gasped as they peered out the windows. Descending on the Manège was an army of eight thousand citizens—tradesmen, working women with children in tow, craftsmen, porters—armed with pikes, pitchforks, old muskets, or whatever they could find. Amid the deputies' futile cries for order, the crowd burst into the room. And for several hours the haranguing continued.

The demonstrators did not stay at the Manège, however. After marching through and presenting a petition to the deputies, they set off for their goal—the Tuileries. At four in the afternoon a group burst through an unlocked side door in the royal palace. They surged through its vast array of rooms, smashing through doors with pikes and hatchets, until they found the King.

Crude insults mingled with wild shouts of "No veto! No priests!" Despite the chaos, Louis remained calm and composed. He obediently donned a red cap, symbol of the Revolution. When a bottle of wine was thrust his way, he drank to the health of the crowd and the nation. But he determinedly refused to budge from his position on the clergy and the protection of Paris. The sans-culottes' first major uprising had failed.

As word got out about the humiliating treatment to which the King had been subjected, the public's sympathy for the demonstrators waned. But the setback was only a temporary one. In fact, before summer was out, the Tuileries Palace would once again be the scene of a riot—a conflagration that would make the events of June 20 seem but a hasty rehearsal.

La Patrie en Danger

In the countryside, cities and villages had begun to take the law into their own hands. Across the land groups of National Guardsmen, who had planned to help form the army of twenty thousand called for by the Assembly, decided to flout the King's veto and set out for Paris on their own.

Then, to add to the tension, the troops on the front suffered several defeats, and Austria began to issue threats. The Assembly had to act.

"*La patrie en danger!* (The country is in danger!)" With these words on July 11 a state of emergency was declared. All men able to bear arms were called to come to the aid of their country, and soon volunteers were descending on the capital by the hundreds.

The Guardsmen from Marseilles were singing a rousing new song as they made their way north. The spirit of urgency and militarism it conjured up was spreading as quickly as the new song itself. Entitled the "Marseillaise," it would one day be the national anthem of all France. Once in Paris, Guardsmen were welcomed by members of the sectional assemblies, and the city's cafés were once again packed.

The July 14 celebration of 1792, a far cry from the grand events of the two years before, was almost lost in the mounting crisis. As before, there was a procession of soldiers and citizens, but this time the Queen was near tears as she watched from the royal balcony. This year, when the King made his way to the Altar of the Nation to take the oath of loyalty, a restless crowd pressed so near him that Marie Antoinette screamed out in fright. And as Louis walked away, only a few feeble cries of "Long live the King!" punctured the heavy silence. It would be his last major public appearance.

By the end of the month the movement to dethrone the King was out in the open. Petition after petition passed before the Assembly. The sectional assemblies, whose delegates were hosting the radical Guardsmen, began meeting daily. Their numbers swelled as one by one they began admitting nonvoting citizens to their ranks. And new, more radical leaders began to meet secretly to plot an advance on the palace.

One of the more radical sections, the "Quinze-vingts," declared its intention to march on the Tuileries Palace on Sunday, August 5, and invited the city's forty-seven other sections to join it. Meanwhile, the Assembly had been working tirelessly to avoid the coming collision. They pleaded with the sections to put off their march until they had had a chance to appease the radicals and dethrone Louis themselves. But for the bourgeois delegates and the Constitution they represented, the clock was running out.

Here Rouget de Lisle is shown singing for the first time the song he composed to be used as a marching tune by French troops about to embark on a campaign against Austria. The song, which was popularized by *fédérés* from Marseilles, became known as the "Marseillaise," and eventually became the French national anthem. The uplifting opening lines, "Let us go, children of the fatherland, / The day of glory has arrived!" and the rousing chorus, "To arms, citizens! / Form your batallions! / Let us march! Let us march!" have inspired Frenchmen and -women for two hundred years. *Cultural Services of the French Embassy.*

The March on the Tuileries

On August 9 the Assembly closed its session—still without having taken action on the fate of the King. Hours later, at midnight, the sound of bells and drum rolls filled the city streets. The signal had been given. Section delegates stormed into the Hôtel de Ville and threw out the councilors. In their place they created a new "Insurrectionary Commune." (In France, the word "commune" was used to describe a self-governing city.)

The next day, August 10, dawned hot and humid. The sun had not been up long before an army of twenty thousand shopkeepers, weavers, and workers began their march on the Tuileries. Up in the royal chambers the King and Queen listened as the tumult of shrieks and abuse grew steadily louder. Louis's face was ashen. Marie Antoinette's eyes were wild and terror-stricken. An adviser counseled the pair to flee to the Assembly, where there might be some hope of protection. At last, after an agony of indecision, Louis had to admit they would not be able to hold out where they were. "Let's go," he said, and he, his wife, and his children made their way for the Manège. They would never see the inside of the palace again.

At the Assembly the royal family was ushered into a small room normally used by note takers. There they cowered, heads bowed, as the sound of muskets and cannons began to mingle with the shouting in the streets.

Central Paris at the time of the Revolution

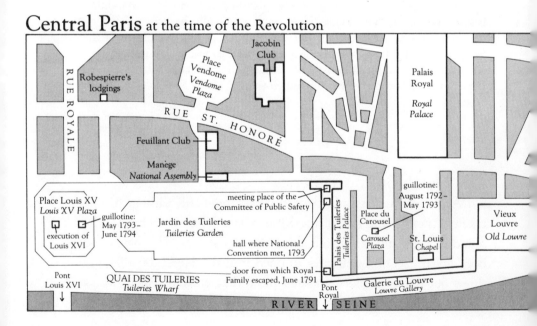

Back at the Tuileries, fierce fighting had broken out between the Swiss guards, loyal to the King, and National Guardsmen. Cries of "Death to the traitors!" filled the air as a contingent of the wild Marseillais pushed through the musket fire and the mob swept through the palace. No one was spared—servants and cooks as well as soldiers met ghoulish ends as ransackers looted and pillaged the rooms. By nightfall over a thousand lay dead.

While the fighting was going on at the Tuileries, the Assembly was at last voting on the future of the monarchy. Under the press of events they decided to suspend the King from his functions, hold him and his family prisoner, and summon a new governing body—a National Convention—which was to be elected by all the men of the nation, not just those with property.

Overnight the face of Paris changed. A new, even more radical Commune had taken over its government. The gates out of the city were shut. Aristocrats who had not managed to escape went into hiding, and foreign countries recalled their ambassadors. The *ancien régime* had truly come to an end. So, too, it seemed, had the bourgeois society that for a brief two years had succeeded it. The era of the French people, of true democracy, had begun.

CHAPTER

4

Chronology

1792

September 2–6	September massacres
September 21	Convention meets for the first time monarchy abolished Republic declared Year I begins
fall	rift grows between radical Jacobins and Girondins French military victories
November 19	France offers military aid to all peoples attempting to recover their liberty
December	trial of the King

•

1793

January 21	Louis XVI executed
winter	France goes to war with England, the Netherlands, and Spain
March	conservative revolt in Vendée begins
spring	protests by *enragés*, radical sans-culottes
April 6	Committee of Public Safety and Revolutionary Tribunal established
May 4	law passed setting maximum prices for grain
May 28	sans-culottes establish new Commune in Paris
May 29–June 2	Girondins ousted from Convention and arrested

Chapter Four:
The Death of the King and the Rise of the People

A boisterous crowd gathered around the table, all eyes intent on the maze of dominoes wending its way between coffee cups and lemonade glasses. Young workingmen mingled with newspaper editors and printers. Every few minutes a loud cheer could be heard—one of the players had cut off his opponent. The Café Procope was dark, with no mirrors or gilt to reflect the light. Still, the sun flooding through the front windows gave the place a warm, homey feel.

Not two decades earlier, in the 1770s, the crowd had been of a different nature. Here Voltaire had come to discuss ideas over a cup of coffee; here Denis Diderot and others had toiled over the famous *Encyclopedia*. In days gone by café chatter included discussions of the latest literary work or philosophical treatise.

In 1792 the Café Procope, located in the heart of the Cordeliers district of Paris, was one of the unofficial centers of revolutionary activity. The incessant games of dominoes were frequently left unfinished when messengers arrived with pieces of urgent information. The café's clientele was changing, and this change reflected the changing nature of those who were powering the Revolution.

By August 1792 a new group was coming into its own. Those who resided in the Cordeliers district and frequented the Café Procope

were typical of it. Although a large number of the men in the district—
over one third—were involved in the printing industry or in jour-
nalism, Cordeliers residents still thought of their district as "working
class." Many had received the same classical educations as had such
earlier revolutionary leaders as the Abbé Sieyès or the Marquis de
Lafayette, but they had dropped the old refinement and intellectualism
in favor of a rough-and-ready, bold, and direct manner. No one better
personified this new class of revolutionaries than Georges-Jacques
Danton.

Domino games at the Procope were accompanied by choruses of
oaths and exclamations; customers were used to knots of spectators
doing all they could to support their favorites with boos and cheers.
But when a certain voice boomed out "Bravo!" heads seven tables
away would turn to see who had spoken. It was a man of a bull-like
build, with a scarred and pockmarked face almost frightening in its
ugly intensity. Vitality emanated from his every pore.

The man was Georges-Jacques Danton. Since his youth Danton
had been a man of tremendous energy, a man who loved life and
plunged into it headfirst. Boyhood adventuresomeness had led him
into several tangles with farm animals, leaving his face disfigured. Yet
he never lost his love for the earthy life of the countryside. Throughout
his years in Paris, even at the height of the Revolution, he maintained
a home in Arcis-sur-Aube, the village of his childhood, and returned
there regularly.

Danton did well at his studies, although he was impatient with the
details of scholarship. He never bothered to develop his penmanship,
and as a result his handwriting was so poor that he disqualified himself
from work as a clerk. In fact, he lacked patience for writing in general
and preferred to rely on his memory and inspiration. Also, when he
spoke, Danton refused to use the literary style expected of one with
his education and threw aside allusions to Latin and Greek classics in
favor of the simple, spontaneous expressions of common people.

As a young lawyer on the way up in Paris, Danton immersed himself

Georges Jacques Danton, the powerful leader of the Cordeliers section, tried to forge unity between the various revolutionary groups. *Culver Pictures, Inc.*

in the pleasures of the city. He frequented cafés and found the rowdy talk and gaming of these public gathering spots thoroughly to his liking.

In spite of his taste for the city's night life, Danton managed to make a good living. In a time when many of the city's young lawyers struggled along in dusty garrets, Danton and his wife were always able to lay a nice spread. His success was largely due to his bold, direct approach to problems. He had a knack for cutting through complex legal arguments and getting things done. His simple manner soon endeared him to the people and inspired their trust. So when the inhabitants of the Cordeliers district began to come to life politically, it was most natural that they should turn for leadership to Georges Danton.

"Boldness, and again boldness and always boldness":
The September Massacres

After August 10 Danton found himself in a unique position of power and influence. He had been appointed Minister of Justice in the Legislative Assembly (which would remain in power until elections to the new National Convention could be held); he was thus the only minister who could claim influence with the new Paris Commune, which had been formed in the wake of the August 10 uprising, as well as with the national government. Through Danton and his powerful influence the spirit of the people might begin to seep into the national government.

Just what would this new reign of the common people be like? Within a month of the August takeover the nation would have a grisly foretaste of what lay in store.

The Assembly had lost many of its more conservative members in the wake of the events of August 10. Now it began to pass a series of radical measures. The King was suspended from his duties, and elections—open to all adult males—were called to choose the new national government, the Convention. Priests who did not support the Constitution were ordered to leave the country. Émigré property, which had been seized by the government in late July, was now ordered put on the market. Perhaps most important of all, all remaining feudal dues were abolished.

Yet, for the people of Paris, even this was not enough. The streets buzzed with rumors of plots by royalists, priests, and other counterrevolutionaries. Soon news that seemed to confirm people's deepest dreads—of foreign and counterrevolutionary attacks—began to filter into the capital. In the western region known as the Vendée, conservative peasants had staged a royalist revolt. Several cities surrendered to invading foreign troops, and word came that Paris itself would soon be vulnerable to attack. Soon people were looking for counterrevolutionaries in every dark corner.

On September 2 Danton rose in the Assembly, and his bass voice at once hushed every nervous whisperer. "When the tocsin sounds," he boomed out, "it will not be a signal of alarm, but the signal to charge against the enemies of our country. . . . To defeat them, gentlemen, we need boldness, and again boldness and always boldness; and France will then be saved."

The people of Paris more than rose to the occasion. Danton had in mind boldness on the battlefield. But many in Paris believed that bold measures were just as necessary right in Paris. Citizens were convinced that the city's prisons were full of counterrevolutionaries who were secretly plotting to help the invading troops.

"Let the blood of the traitors flow!" cried one journalist, and the rest of the city's radical press echoed his cry. Within hours of Danton's impassioned speech in the Assembly, the gutters of Paris had already begun to run with blood. Priests being held captive in a convent were brutally hacked to death. Gangs of citizens armed with pikes, swords, and hatchets stormed into the city's prisons and, after brief "trials" that made a mockery of the word, proceeded to do away with anyone

who could in the least be suspected of counterrevolutionary sentiments. As the days wore on, carts bearing mounds of corpses began
to wend their way through the streets. And by September 7 over a
thousand prisoners were dead.

Danton's role in the massacres was typical of the one he would play
in the crucial months ahead. He stood with the radicals, yet was open
to building bridges to the other revolutionary factions. Did he actually
mastermind the murders? We do not know. He certainly did not try
to stop them—perhaps afraid of losing his favored standing with the
sans-culottes. Yet Danton also worked to prevent prisoners from outside Paris from being brought into the city, and when radical leaders
grew suspicious of the Girondin leaders who had made feeble attempts
to talk the crowds out of their bloody attacks, Danton personally
intervened to defend the Girondins.

Characters in the Revolutionary Drama: *Jean-Paul Marat*

In his well-known *Notes from the Underground,* the great Russian
novelist Dostoyevsky wrote about a political radical who lived
in a dingy basement room. The wild lifestyles of young activists
of the 1960s have often been commented on. Many would trace
this traditional association of political radicalism and unconven-
tional lifestyles to the French Revolution. Actually, despite their
zealousness, many of the men who led the revolt of the third
estate were notable for the normalcy of their behavior and their
private lives. Danton prided himself on his hospitality and his
wine cellar and liked to invite friends over to dine. Robespierre
was always immaculately groomed, his wig always properly powdered, his cravat tied just so. There were some, however, who
were definitely prototypes for later "wild radicals." For perhaps
no one would this be more true than for Jean-Paul Marat.

Marat was apt to impress anyone who caught a glimpse of him as a man possessed. His face was sallow, his eyes green, his near-black hair stringy from lack of washing. He regularly wore tattered and dirty clothing. Often those who stood close to him were likely to notice that he smelled. Marat even bragged about his impatience with personal hygiene and health measures, though he also suffered from a painful skin disease that he could soothe only with warm water. He boasted of spending only two hours a day between sleeping, eating, dressing, and other household affairs. His rooms were meagerly furnished with an iron bedstead and a minimal number of other functional pieces. After he had been threatened with arrest in April 1793, Marat and his mistress took to the sewers of Paris. But whereas most men would have surfaced as soon as the danger had passed, Marat seemed to revel in his underground life. In fact, he continued to dwell in the dank and dark, companion to the city's many rats, for months longer than was necessary.

Marat not only posed as a persecuted man. He thought like one as well. At one point he had led a reasonably open and upstanding life. He was trained as a doctor and in England had practiced medicine and written scientific papers of such merit that he was granted an honorary degree. At one time he lived in an elegantly appointed drawing room, complete with silk curtains and a chandelier. But after a while Marat's life became shadier. For several years there is little record of his doings, save some indications that he had run into debt. We do know, however, that the French Academy refused him any recognition for his work, and that this snub had a deep impact on him. From that point on Marat's suspicions that others had it in for him simply grew and deepened. He assumed, on behalf of the nation, the same attitude of distrust and defensiveness that he had for himself.

Not long after the Revolution broke out in 1789, Marat began

Jean-Paul Marat, in his journal *The Friend of the People,* gave voice to many of the radical sentiments of the people. He was more concerned, however, with the effects his writing would produce than with truth and accuracy. "You should have seen the casual way in which he composed his articles," wrote one man who had visited Marat as he was straining to meet a deadline. "Without knowing anything about some public man, he would ask the first person he met what he thought of him and write it down." *Culver Pictures, Inc.*

to publish the small, eight-page newspaper known as *The Friend of the People*. The paper appeared daily, and in almost every issue one or another well-known figure was exposed as a traitor, a danger to the country. And Marat was uncompromising in his proposal as to what to do with such traitors: "I believe in the cutting off of heads," he remarked at one point. It was he alone who publicly stood by his role in the grisly slaughter of the September massacres. "In order to ensure public tranquility, two hundred thousand heads must be cut off," he said.

Ultimately Marat ended up distrusting even the people with whom he claimed to be friends. "O Parisians," he wrote, "you frivolous, feeble, and cowardly folk . . . you who have a rage for liberty as though it were a new fashion in clothes . . . you whose only incentive is vanity, and whom nature might have formed for the highest destinies, if she had only given you judgment and perseverance—must you always be treated as grown-up children?"

To that last question Marat would answer yes. Unlike most of the other radicals, he had no faith that the people could govern themselves. He never let up in his criticisms of those in power. Yet he would sooner have seen a dictator take over the reins than see power go to the people. In fact, he actually proposed a dictatorship.

Despite his venomous pen, Marat truly loved the common people. In an account of how he spent his time, he judged that at least six hours of each day were spent simply listening to the grievances of his fellow citizens. The people sensed this love and returned it in an unswerving loyalty. When he was found "not guilty" of the charge of attacking the Girondins, the crowds swarmed around him, swooped him up onto their shoulders, and, cheering, carried him back to the hall of the Convention.

After his brutal murder by Charlotte Corday, a Girondin sympathizer, Marat was given a hero's funeral. The procession lasted seven hours. And in the months following he achieved the status of a martyr. Plays and poems were written about him. Streets were named after him. Children were taught to make the sign of the cross in his name.

Marat's reputation has varied greatly in the years after his death. He has been denounced as a villain and held up as a liberator of the people. But whatever one's opinion of the man, it would be hard to deny that he was one of the Revolution's most colorful characters.

Danton had a knack for playing the go-between. As Paris became increasingly polarized there would be a desperate need for such a talent.

Jacobin and Girondin

In the aftermath of August 10 and the September massacres, the lines among the various revolutionary groups were more sharply drawn than ever. Despite the radical measures passed by the Assembly, the men of the Paris Commune remained deeply suspicious of the national government. The Commune demanded that Louis be dethroned and tried. For most members of the Assembly this was too hasty and crude a measure.

In facing the Commune the national government itself could not present a united front. It was torn apart by a conflict so great that it dwarfed all else for months of revolutionary history. This was the historic conflict between the Jacobins and the Girondins.

The nation had gone to the polls. By the third week in September 1792, the 749 newly elected deputies were called to meet. Just what sort of men had the people chosen to represent them this time?

The two most influential groups among the new deputies were the Girondins and Jacobins. Both shared a republican outlook. There was nearly universal enthusiasm for the first act of the Convention—the declaration of September 21 that the monarchy had been abolished. But there the similarity ended.

One hundred sixty-five of the new representatives were Girondins. The Girondins in the new National Convention were very like those of the Assembly; in fact many of the old deputies had been reelected. As a group they tended to be well educated and cultured and, if not rich, at least accustomed to the company of those with money. Sympathy for the needs of the common people did not come easily to them. Also, many of the Girondins were from the provinces—one more reason they tended to be suspicious of the rowdy citizens of the capital city.

The radical Jacobins were not all common folk; many of them were lawyers. Yet they tended to be a more colorful group than did the more genteel Girondins. In addition to Danton, there was Jean-Paul Marat, a swarthy and intense man, formerly a doctor, who now found himself forever on the wrong side of the law, and whose life was devoted to producing his scathing revolutionary journal *The Friend of the People.* There was also the formidable Robespierre, whose icy, bespectacled stare and passion for impeccably tailored suits were well-known trademarks. The Jacobins even called attention to themselves by where they sat in the Assembly. They all gathered on the highest benches in the hall, located just to the left of the President's desk. For this they came to be called, collectively, the "Mountain."

Even though they were not themselves truly "of the people," the Jacobins' sympathies were inclined to lie with the common men and women of the nation or, more particularly, with the working people of the nation's capital. The difference between the two factions had first shown up in the split over the issue of the war against Austria, Prussia, and the other monarchist nations. While the Girondins had been enthusiastic in their support of the war, the Jacobins had opposed it. The Jacobins claimed that the King's support was a sure sign that it could not possibly be in the best interests of the common citizen. After the events of August and early September, the split grew steadily more pronounced. Most Jacobins supported the massacres. The Girondins, on the other hand, became increasingly fierce in their condemnation of the massacres as the weeks passed. There were sharp differences over the role of the new Paris Commune as well. Many of the new Jacobin delegates were from Paris, and they were fiercely supportive of that city's new government. Girondins, on the other hand, tended to be distrustful.

Bitter, personal quarrels heightened the division between the two groups. Back in October 1792 Robespierre, up to that time one of the regulars at the Rolands' salon, suddenly stopped coming. Madame Roland, who had a special fondness for her idealistic guest, felt personally betrayed, and it was not long afterward that her husband blasted Robespierre in the Assembly. Other Girondins, suspecting Robespierre of plans to have them killed in the September massacres, joined in the attacks.

But it was the Girondins' quarrel with Danton that was most vicious and hateful. Madame Roland from the beginning had taken a strong personal dislike to Danton. Accustomed to the courtly attentions of the men at her salon, she found his rough-and-ready ways deeply distasteful. The Rolands and others accused Danton of aspiring to become a dictator. At first Danton rebuffed the attacks. In an impassioned speech to the Assembly, he made clear his own opposition to dictatorship. "If there is any man so vile as to want to rule despotically over the representatives of the people, his head will fall the moment he is unmasked," he declared. He followed with a plea for an end to the quarrels: "Anyone who tries to destroy the unity of France must die." But his attempts to forge unity met with little success. The Girondin attacks continued and grew to encompass all of Paris. The patience of Danton and others was wearing thin.

Characters in the Revolutionary Drama: *Women in the Revolution*

The October 1789 march on Versailles consisted largely of women. The most influential Girondin salon was run by a woman, Madame Roland. It was women rioting in bakeries and grocers' shops that gave strength to the sans-culotte movement in Paris in 1793. And later that year the radical leader Marat was murdered by a woman. From the beginning women figured prominently in the French Revolution. But just what was the nature of their role?

For the most part women supported the plans and efforts of the men who were leading the revolt of the third estate. There were exceptions. A few women, such as Olympe de Gouge, pushed to secure for women the right to vote and serve in government.

In addition bourgeois women in many cities formed their own revolutionary clubs. At first the activities of these groups resembled those of many other traditional women's clubs. They worked to provide aid for the poor by such means as running lotteries. They also helped one another to set a good revolutionary example—as by attending only Masses said by priests supportive of the Revolution.

Such quiet, sedate activities were eventually supplanted by others of so total and intense a nature that they often put the efforts of men to shame. The deepening of women's involvement coincided with the outbreak of the war in 1792. All across France the women's clubs worked to collect linens for soldiers' bandages. In one town twenty thousand pounds of sheets were collected. This figure is even more impressive when it is remembered that a woman's linens were often her dowry, one of her most prized and valuable possessions, intended to last for life. In another country town the women contributed their wedding rings to be pawned to raise funds to purchase clothing for the soldiers. Other groups armed themselves and prepared to raise defenses of their own if needed. And all over, women pledged to rid their towns of traitors at home while their husbands fought the enemies abroad. The intensity of their efforts was such that some of their menfolk were even alarmed. One official compared women revolutionaries to tigresses and vultures eager for blood.

Although they were a minority, some women during the Revolution fought for greater rights for their sex. Chief among these aims were the right to divorce and the right to a better education. Above is one artist's rendition of a liberated Frenchwoman. *Cultural Services of the French Embassy.*

The women's clubs also stepped up their activities on yet another front—that of economics. The clubs supplied a number of the principal voices speaking out in support of fixed prices. In fact, in the area of economics, women revolutionaries led the way from the beginning. It was chiefly women who had participated in the march on Versailles, and chiefly sans-culotte women who had raided Parisian grocery stores in 1792.

This area was left to the women as part of a traditional recognition of the lower-class woman's responsibility to help provide for her family. It was accepted that a laboring man could not make enough to provide for more than a wife and one or possibly two children, and that the support of an average-size family would require the contribution of the wife as well. So women of the third estate traditionally worked. Unmarried girls worked as servants. Married women worked at home as spinners, lacemakers (an enormous home industry), dressmakers, embroiderers, and corsetieres.

The Revolution had done away with much work in the garment industry, which had been patronized largely by the clergy and the aristocracy. This, coupled with dramatic increases in food prices due to poor harvests, made it almost inevitable that women would turn to more drastic measures to feed their families. And the men seemed quite willing to leave much of the rioting to them.

Certainly in this area women were leaders. Yet this is about the only area in which revolutionary women were allowed so important a role. The vision of a liberated society, which captured French imaginations for five years, was largely that of a liberated *male* society. There was an important minority that tried to get women to see that they were accepting a subservient role in their families. But for the most part even the most prominent of revolutionary women, such as the brilliant Madame Roland, willingly accommodated themselves to backseat roles.

In fact, with the triumph of the radical Jacobins and their vision of a renewed and virtuous society, the place allotted to women was actually reduced. In the fall of 1793 the Convention ordered all revolutionary women's clubs closed. Gatherings of women were considered decadent and frivolous—and were associated with the *ancien regime.* The role of a proper revolutionary wife, the government said, was to keep a comfortable and inviting home for her menfolk to return to after hard work at their civic duties.

The French Revolution left the Western world many important legacies in the area of human rights. But, despite the important contributions women made to the Revolution, rights for women were not prominent among these. Surely seeds of a new consciousness had been sown, but it would remain for later generations of Frenchwomen to see them come to fruition.

By early November what little remained in the Convention of dignified parliamentary debate had degenerated to a state of near anarchy. Jacobins repeatedly interrupted speakers with whom they disagreed. Appeals were constantly being made to the spectators in the galleries. Legislation was slowed by demands for roll call votes, and debates regularly turned into name-calling contests. Finally the question of what to do about the King brought matters to a crisis point.

The Death of the King

The rooms were a far cry from either Versailles or the Tuileries. The walls were filled with graffiti, the floors dank and cold. Doors were fastened with large locks. Here for four months Louis and Marie Antoinette and their children had made their home. For weeks now the King had passed the long days reading and doing lessons with his children, the Queen in knitting and embroidering, and the children making do as best they could with a few games. Once a day they were allowed a walk—often taken in the company of guards who taunted them along the way. But for Louis this dreary existence would soon come to an end.

The Jacobins were calling for action about the King in ever more strident tones. Not only did most have no hesitation about calling for a trial; some even called for execution without a trial. On November 13 a fanatical young deputy only twenty-five years old, Louis-Antoine Léon de Saint-Just, opened the debate on the fate of the King by calling for his execution as an enemy of the state. (Danton, true to his role of independent thinker and mediator, did not support the

When Louis XVI was beheaded on January 21, 1793, twenty thousand soldiers were stationed in Paris to keep order. Although the King's last words were obscured by the tapping of the drums, some reports recorded them as "I forgive those who are guilty of my death, and I pray God that the blood which you are about to shed may never be required of France." *Bibliothèque Nationale (Art Resource/Lauros-Giraudon).*

radical course proposed by his fellow Jacobins. He feared that the death of Louis would endanger France's position in the struggle with Austria, Prussia, and the other allies.)

Throughout November the Girondins struggled valiantly to avert a trial. Then, late in the month, a cupboard of the King's was discovered that contained correspondence with a secret agent and other evidence that showed he was attempting to assist counterrevolutionary forces. There was little left to debate. A trial was set to begin in early December.

After weeks of lengthy, impassioned speeches, the case finally came to a close. Both sides were given a week to print up and distribute their arguments. On January 14 the galleries of the convention hall at the Manège were packed with people from all walks of life. The shrill voices of Parisian fishmongers mingled with the hushed whispers of lawyers and journalists. Many had brought fruit and wine to sustain them through the long deliberations. The voting would be by roll call—a measure the Jacobins had insisted on, as it would allow all in the galleries to identify "traitors" to the Revolution.

One by one the deputies solemnly mounted the tribune and announced their votes. Some deputies took leave to go out and eat. Others asked friends to wake them, then dozed. It was nearly five days before the process was complete. The final verdict was that Louis was guilty of conspiracy. The King was to die. The Girondins had tried two last desperate measures to stave off the terrible deed—first requesting that the decision be referred to the people at large for a vote, and then requesting a stay of execution. Both proposals were defeated.

Shortly before dawn on January 20, 1793, Louis was awakened and informed of the dread decision. The date of execution, he was told, was set for the next day. The King remained calm and composed, keeping the terrible news to himself for as long as he could. By evening the time had come to tell his family. Moved by the wailing and sobbing of his wife and children, Louis too broke down and wept for the agony that lay ahead for his loved ones.

But by the following morning he had regained his composure. He did not flinch even when a drumroll announcing the day's solemn event started up outside his window. After requesting a final blessing, Louis strode deliberately out to the carriage that awaited him. As the carriage passed slowly through the city streets, silent eyes peered intently through a gray drizzle for a last look at the former ruler. By nine thirty the carriage had reached the foot of the terrible platform on which the stanchions and icy steel blade of the guillotine had been erected.

Slowly, still with dignity, Louis mounted the platform. He asked for the drums to stop in order that he might address the crowd. But he had scarcely begun to speak when the drums took up again and drowned out his last words. And then, within minutes, a young guard was hoisting a grisly head aloft for all to see.

Politics of the People: The Enragés

The execution of the King was to be one of the last important acts of the National Convention. The Convention itself would continue to meet for months to come. Yet within weeks of the beheading, its sessions were regularly deadlocked by the continuing contest between Jacobin and Girondin. The Jacobins' push for Louis's execution had made them popular with the people of Paris. Yet they remained only a minority in the government. The majority, led by the Girondins, still had their supporters. The French army had boasted several heartening victories early in 1793, and as the leading general, Charles-François Dumouriez, was a Girondin, this success had won sympathy for them. The Girondins also remained popular with many of the people in the provinces, who were consistently more conservative than those of the nation's capital. But the Girondins' lack of unity cost them power in the Convention.

As the government became more and more ineffectual, the people of Paris increasingly took matters into their own hands.

On February 25 women all over the capital stormed into grocers' shops, took over the stores, and sold their contents off at prices working people could more readily afford. All the while, they shouted for the fixing of prices and the punishment of food hoarders. The people wanted more than political freedom. They wanted economic security. Harvests had been bad, and food and other goods increasingly were used for the soldiers on the front. As they had for some time, working people demanded that the government fix prices to help end spiraling inflation. Although government regulation of prices had been commonplace in earlier times, to the revolutionaries such a measure was, ironically, quite radical. One of the chief beliefs of Enlightenment thinkers was the necessity of a free market. The philosophes and those who took their cues from them believed as strongly in a free market as they did in political freedom. Not even the radical men of the Mountain were prepared to go so far as to support government price-fixing. And so, led by a radical priest named Jacques Roux and a postal worker, Jean Varlet, sans-culottes in Paris and a few other large cities began to demonstrate on their own. In addition to price controls, these men and women called for a tax on wealthy citizens to raise the money needed for the war. They also called for the elimination of all Girondins from the Convention. To some these propositions seemed so radical that they earned the agitators the nickname *enragés*, meaning "madmen."

Bad news on the military front gave the frustrated *enragés* just the leverage they needed. Back in the fall of 1792 French troops had had a series of victories against the Austrian and Prussian forces. Buoyed by their success the Girondins had expanded the scope of the war; no longer just a defense against the enemies of the French revolutionary government, it became a crusade on behalf of oppressed people in all nations. In November the National Convention declared that "in the name of the French nation . . . [they would] bring fraternity and aid to all peoples that wish[ed] to recover their liberty." Naturally, this policy was a challenge to all the monarchs of Europe. The execution of the King was the last straw. By February France was at war with England, the Netherlands, and Spain, as well as with its earlier enemies.

To meet the nation's increased need for defense, the Convention called for a draft of three hundred thousand new recruits. Every unmarried man of sound body between the ages of eighteen and forty was eligible. But the government had great difficulty meeting the quota it had set. In the Vendée, where people had already shown their antagonism to the revolutionary government, the citizens resisted violently. Conservative Catholicism was still strong there, and men were loath to help defend a Revolution the Pope had condemned. By

March the nation was suffering on battlefields both at home and abroad. A surprise attack on the Netherlands had backfired, and French troops were badly beaten. And at home a full-blown civil war raged in the Vendée. To top things off, the nation's leading general, the headstrong Dumouriez, deserted to the Austrians.

The nation desperately needed sans-culotte manpower. Perhaps now the men in power would be ready to listen more seriously to their requests.

An Arena of Gladiators: The Sans-Culottes Enter the Jacobin-Girondin Struggle

Out of concern for the welfare of the nation and out of desire for political power, the Jacobins began to court the sans-culotte troops of the Paris sections. As one of them put it, "If you want the poor to help you make the Revolution a reality, it is absolutely essential to keep them alive." Up to this point Georges Danton had been using his influence to try to hold the Convention together as a unified body. "Let bygones be bygones," he said to one of the Girondins. But when his efforts only met with defiance, he threw his support behind the Jacobins. "I was wrong," his huge voice boomed. "I now abandon moderation because prudence has its limits. . . ." Danton now joined Robespierre in declaring that the nation's safety depended on the assistance of the common people.

Some of the common people's requests were answered by emergency measures passed by the Convention in the wake of the military reverses. The government set up a new governing body called the Committee of Public Safety to watch over the actions of the ministers of the Convention, many of whom were Girondins. It had also created a Revolutionary Tribunal, or court, whose purpose was to try and to punish counterrevolutionaries; it established "surveillance committees" in each city to keep an eye on local foreigners and declared stiff new penalties for rebels and a tax on the rich.

The new governing bodies, with their careful monitoring for rebels and wayward Girondin ministers, certainly seemed to meet the demands of the *enragés*. But there was a hitch. There was no assurance that the new committees and Tribunal would be in the hands of men sympathetic to the people. The sans-culottes demanded that the Convention be purged of Girondins. Within days of the passage of the emergency measures, a struggle more furious than ever followed in the Convention. Both the Jacobins and the Girondins accused one another of royalist plots. Name-calling, vile speech, boos, and jeers became the order of the day in the Convention. In Danton's words, it was an "arena of gladiators."

The Girondins lashed out by striking at one of the most fiery and controversial of the Jacobin leaders—Jean-Paul Marat. In March Marat's controversial journal, *The Friend of the People*, had issued a dramatic call for the arrest of all the Girondins in the Convention. The Girondins, in turn, had Marat brought before the Revolutionary Tribunal.

Their scheme backfired. The Tribunal was sympathetic to the radicals and found Marat not guilty. After Marat's victory the Convention was besieged by petitions to unseat the Girondins. In an atmosphere of mounting tension the Jacobins took a major step to ally themselves still more closely with the sans-culotte radicals. They agreed to support the demand for price controls. On May 4 the Convention passed a decree that authorized the nation's cities to establish maximum prices for grain. Meanwhile, the Girondins countered by trying to stir up citizens in the provinces, where suspicion of Paris was common, against the Jacobins. In mid-May they even proposed that the nation's capital and national government be moved out of Paris to Bourges. The proposal to move the Convention was roundly defeated.

From that point on radical and violent action became steadily more common. On May 29 Danton made one final attempt to get the two sides to work together. In a plea made to the Committee of Public Safety he begged the deputies to lay aside their differences. But it was too late. The next day the sans-culottes of Paris took matters into

After being found not guilty of the charges brought against him by the Girondins, Marat was carried back to the meeting hall of the National Convention on the shoulders of his devoted followers. This engraving shows several symbols of the sans-culottes on the bayonets and pikes of the crowd: the full-length pants of the working man; the *bonnet rouge* ("red bonnet"), patterned after a common man's wool cap; and the twin tablets on which the Declaration of the Rights of Man and the Citizen was often printed. *Culver Pictures, Inc.*

their own hands once again. They created a new municipal government in Paris, a revolutionary committee, and drew up a final petition for the arrest of the Girondin deputies. A demonstration was organized for June 2, a Sunday, so that more workingmen would be able to participate.

Sunday morning dawned to the ringing of the alarm bell and the roll of drums. It was not long before thousands of troops supplied by the sections of the city, together with several thousand National

Guardsmen, surrounded the building where the Convention met. A delegation entered and announced to the assembly of delegates that no one would be allowed to leave until the Girondins had been surrendered to the people.

The braver delegates protested. "So long as one is allowed to speak freely here," said one, "I will not let the character of representative of the people be degraded in my person." Then the deputies decided that they would simply leave. They rose proudly and walked outside. But they were greeted by eighty thousand troops stationed outside the door. There was nowhere they could go. By afternoon the delegates had returned to their seats and reluctantly voted for the arrest of twenty-two Girondin deputies.

The long, bitter struggle between Jacobin and Girondin had at last come to an end. Danton's dream of a united revolution had finally been achieved. The people were now "one." But this had not come about as the great leader of the people had hoped, through the method of compromise and reconciliation. Instead, this new unity was the result of force and violence. This was a shift of grave significance, the herald of a year both France and the world would long remember.

Setting the Scene:
The Guillotine

Knots of people waving tricolor flags hung out of the windows. Still greater throngs lined the streets. At the base of the scaffold itself, the crowds were thicker and louder still. There, men and women, boys and girls vied with one another for the best vantage point. All were eagerly awaiting the executions of the day. Some had even made a day's outing of the spectacle, bringing with them their knitting or lunch.

As the cart bearing the condemned passed by, a great roar went up. There was a slight hush as a drumroll was sounded and

In this drawing of the execution of the Girondin Jacques Pierre Brissot and his accomplices, the various stages of a guillotining are shown. The victims, their hands tied, were wheeled in carts called tumbrils to the Place de la Revolution, where the guillotine was erected. *Bibliothèque Nationale (Art Resource/Lauros-Giraudon)*.

the first prisoner, head shorn, hands bound, and face pale with fright, was led up the steps to the platform where the guillotine stood. Slowly, its cold steel glistening in the sun, the huge blade was hoisted to the top of the pillars. Then—*crash!*

It was all over in a split second—a moment almost lost amid the cheering and the jostling of the spectators eager to get a glimpse of the bloody head before it was tossed into the basket that was waiting for it.

To us such a spectacle, such a method of punishment, seems gruesome and horrible. Actually, the guillotine, which was first used in France during the Revolution, was an important step forward in the transformation of Western ideas about crime and punishment.

In the seventeenth and eighteenth centuries—indeed, for many centuries prior—the punishments set forth for most crimes in France were physical, painful, and public. Dozens of crimes were punishable by death. And people were condemned to die in a variety of ways, the degree of suffering induced depending on the seriousness of the offense. An ordinance of 1670 included the following: hanging, having one's hands cut off or tongue cut out and then being hanged, being broken on a wheel, being strangled and then broken, being burned, being drawn apart by four horses, and having one's head cut off. Even lesser crimes were often punished by inflicting pain. Flogging and branding were common penalties.

The guillotine represented a step in a new direction. First introduced to France in 1792, the guillotine consisted of a large, heavy knife blade that could be raised and allowed to fall between two grooved posts connected at the top by a crossbar. Guided by the grooves and speeded by its weight, the knife blade fell with such force and precision that it neatly severed the head of anyone positioned beneath it. Death by guillotine was instantaneous and thus nearly painless.

In fact, painlessness was the point of the machine. The name given this beheading device derives from that of the doctor who first advocated its use—Dr. Joseph-Ignace Guillotin. One of Dr. Guillotin's chief motives in pushing for the passage of a law requiring that all death sentences be carried out by means of the machine was to make the punishment as painless as possible. (Another reason was to make punishment more democratic. Until the Revolution, relatively painless beheadings had been the privilege of criminals of noble birth.)

Of course, the adoption of the guillotine was only a step toward a new approach to punishment. At the time of the Revolution executions were still very much a public spectacle, as were punishments of old. Yet in reading about the gory spectacle that these beheadings became, we are apt to forget that the guillotine represented progress of a kind.

CHAPTER
5
Chronology

Year I   **1793**

early June	provinces protest Jacobin takeover
June 24	new constitution—extends right to vote to all men
July 10	Danton removed from Committee of Public Safety
July 13	Marat murdered
July 27	Robespierre joins Committee of Public Safety
August 13	*levée en masse* declared
September 4–5	Hébertist uprising in Paris terror declared "the order of the day"
September 17	Law of Suspects decreed

(Revolutionary months were not employed for Year I)

Year II

8 Vendémiaire	September 29	fixing of prices and wages
Vendémiaire	late September	de-Christianization begins
Brumaire	October–November	Girondins, many others guillotined
20 Brumaire	November 11	Festival of Reason celebrated in Notre Dame

Year II (continued)

| Frimaire | early December | Danton, Desmoulins, and others move for relaxation of Terror |

•

1794

16 Pluviôse	February 4	slavery abolished in colonies
Ventôse	February	Laws of Ventôse passed to distribute émigré property to poor
Germinal	late March	Hébertists executed
13–17 Germinal	April 2–6	trial and execution of Danton and followers
20 Prairial	June 8	Festival of the Supreme Being
22 Prairial	June 10	Law of 22 Prairial speeds up trials of suspects Great Terror begins
9 Thermidor	July 27	revolt against Robespierre
10 Thermidor	July 28	Robespierre executed

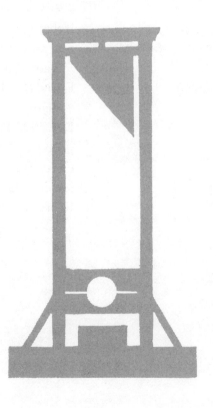

Chapter Five:

The Coming of the Terror

People were no longer called "monsieur" or "madame." These old titles, once the accepted form of polite address for any upstanding bourgeois, were now considered insults, since they had not been employed for working people. Instead, people of all classes were addressed as "Citizen So-and-so." Babies might be named not Marie or Vincent after Christian saints, but Spartacus after an ancient Roman, or Jean-Paul after the revolutionary hero Marat. There were no more Sundays —or Mondays or Tuesdays or Wednesdays. Instead, weeks had ten days, with every tenth day rather than every seventh a day of rest. Those who could still manage to figure out when to go to church were likely to find their local church closed. Their priest, by order of the government, might have resigned his post to marry and turned his vestments over to the nation to be made into uniforms and bandages. There were still festivals, but in place of statues of the Virgin Mary pretty young women posing as "Reason" were carried in procession. In Paris and other large cities a far more common "festival" was that held daily in the public square where the guillotine was erected. The victims of the shiny blade soon numbered as many as three thousand in a month. While at first the victims were mainly émigrés, royalists, and others clearly opposed to the Revolution, they now included those who had once been considered staunch revolutionaries. Madame Roland was guillotined in November 1793. Other victims included Carmelite nuns and women whose alleged crime was that they showed regret when their husbands were guillotined. In one provincial city, when even the guillotine seemed too slow, hundreds of prisoners were drowned en masse.

Traditionally, a revolution is thought of as a political phenomenon—that is, a change in government. Some revolutions, however, are so broad in scope that they overturn and transform every aspect of life. Certainly this was true of the French Revolution. At no time was the total nature of the Revolution more evident than in the year ushered in by the Jacobin coup of May 29–June 2, 1793.

The Death of Moderation and the Rise of Robespierre

In the months immediately following the Jacobin takeover, those in power still pursued a policy of moderation and conciliation. In the provinces those who had long distrusted Paris and who sympathized with the ousted Girondins were hostile to the new government. The Jacobins, concerned about retaining national support, tried to put suspicions to rest.

" . . . Pardon the majority. Mistakes must not be confused with crimes and you have no wish to be severe. The time has come at last when the people may hope for happiness, when liberty is no longer a matter of party faction." These words of peace were addressed to the Convention by the sharp and dapper Saint-Just, who was now one of the principal Jacobins.

But this more moderate stance would not last long. France's military situation was desperate. The Austrians were invading the nation on the northern front, and to the south the Spanish were preparing to do so. Meanwhile, a conservative revolt in the Vendée continued to rage. Rebel troops had actually taken over a number of cities. Citizens were both panicked and outraged. They laid the blame for the military

France at the time of the Revolution

GREAT
BRITAIN

UNITED
PROVINCES

HOLY
ROMAN
EMPIRE

English Channel

○ Cologne

Brussels

AUSTRIAN
NETHERLANDS
(annexed 1793)

○ Coblenz

Mainz
Worms

PICARDIE

Seine R.

Oise R.

Paris

Versailles

Arcis-sur-Aube

Battle of Fleurus

Loire R.

Saône R.

Quiberon Bay

Nantes

Nevers

SWITZERLAND

VENDÉE

*Atlantic
Ocean*

Lyon

SAVOY
*(annexed
1793–4)*

Grenoble

PIEDMONT

Bordeaux

Dordogne R.

NICE
*(annexed
1793–4)*

GIRONDE

Garonne R.

Rhône R.

GARD

AVIGNON
(annexed 1790)

Toulouse

Marseille

Toulon

SPAIN

*Mediterranean
Sea*

situation on the government, accusing it of being too lax with trea-
sonous officers and demanding the vigorous prosecution of traitors.
Desperate over the military situation, the Jacobins were finally pushed
to abandon the moderate policies of their first weeks in power.

When did moderation give way to radicalism? It is hard to pick a
date, but one crucial moment came when Danton was removed from
the Committee of Public Safety and, not long after, Maximilien Robespierre joined it.

Danton and Robespierre are a study in contrasts. Whereas Danton
had such a rough-and-ready demeanor that women sometimes found
him frightening, Robespierre was a small, thin man known for his
fussiness about his dress and toilette. He had his hair set and powdered
daily by a barber long after this had gone out of fashion. He dressed
in immaculate, stylish clothes, favoring such colors as green. Danton
clearly enjoyed the sensual side of life. He loved a good meal and
good wine, especially when shared with friends. He took pleasure in
a game of dominoes and was proud of his inviting home. Robespierre,
by contrast, was a man of simple, even austere personal habits. He
took almost no interest in food, living principally on coffee and fruit.
He never had a home of his own, boarding either with his sister,
another bachelor, or a fellow revolutionary eager to house him. He
took very few breaks from his work, save for occasional walks and,
even more rarely, a trip to the theater to see a tragedy. Danton regularly
roused audiences by the sheer power of his voice. He spoke sponta-
neously, without notes, in the words of ordinary people. His pene-
trating gaze could wither. Robespierre's speeches were studied, his
sentences complex and long, his voice annoyingly grating. Whether
speaking in public or one-on-one, he almost never looked those he
was addressing in the eye.

Maximilien Robespierre is shown here in the immaculately curled and powdered wig for which he was famous. It was said that Robespierre had a horror
of laughter. This portrait captures something of his grave, reserved manner.
French Embassy Press and Information Division.

Characters in the Revolutionary Drama: *Robespierre, the Incorruptible*

"So long as the French Revolution is regarded . . . as the birth of ideas that enlightened the nineteenth [century], and of hopes that still inspire our own age; . . . so long will Robespierre, who lived and died for the Revolution, remain one of the great figures of history." So spoke the respected English historian J. M. Thompson.

Yet a fellow historian, the Frenchman Alphonse Aulard, described the same man as one who "adores and displays his ego" and whose "hatreds are as eternal and inexorable as those of Mme Roland." This wide discrepancy in the judgment of Robespierre's character is typical. From his day to our own, Maximilien Robespierre has been one of the most controversial characters in Western history.

The Incorruptible

The case in Robespierre's favor is well summed up by the word "incorruptible," his nickname even in his own time. Robespierre had an unswerving devotion to virtue. One of the most important virtues, both to Robespierre and to his contemporaries, was freedom from the passion for wealth. The eighteenth century was an era in which corruption among public officials was rampant, even among revolutionaries. Schemes were continually being uncovered in which leaders of the people were turning the Revolution to their own profit. Not so with Robespierre. He enjoyed a few simple luxuries—fine silk stockings, the attentions of a barber, nice clothes, and pastries—but aside from these he lived a simple life. The opportunities to abuse the people's trust were great: Robespierre had control of millions of francs (the new basic coin, about equal to a livre), and could have sold pardons for a handsome price. Yet he lived within his deputy's allowance of eighteen francs a day.

"That man will go far," Mirabeau had remarked of him. "He believes what he says." Another aspect of Robespierre's "incorruptibility" was his unshakable and intensely serious devotion to his ideals. At a young age he came to believe in the goodness and sovereign importance of the common people. He remained faithful to these ideals right up to the end. He kept a copy of Rousseau's *The Social Contract* beside his bed much as other people keep a Bible. Robespierre was never much of a public speaker. When he first appeared before the Convention, his rasping voice and stilted language were such that his speeches were not even heard out. But eventually he was able to hold an audience at rapt attention. This was not so much because of any great improvement in his oratorical skill. Rather, the sincerity with which he spoke of such things as the need for universal voting rights or the evil of the wealthy moved the common people and inspired their devotion. Robespierre was one of the few revolutionaries who would not compromise his principles, and the people loved him for it.

Later generations as well have responded to the intensity and passion of Robespierre's vision. Robespierre was not a great or original thinker. Still, his constant repetition of the theme of equality and his championing of the poor have led at least one major historian to refer to him as one of the apostles of modern democracy.

The Hypocrite

Robespierre genuinely believed that he loved the people. Yet, even in his own day, some doubted the sincerity of this claim. Although he was referred to as "the Incorruptible," some began to accuse him of hypocrisy. In later generations, too, Robespierre's detractors have often focused on what they termed his "hypocrisy." Love of the people was not his dominant passion, people have argued, but rather love of self and envy of others.

The evidence for this claim is strong. From his youth, Robespierre was an isolate. As a student at the prestigious College Louis le Grand he made no real friends. As an adult he had a nervous twitch and seemed uncomfortable in the presence of others; he seldom made eye contact when he was talking to someone, and in his last years was shielded from much interaction by the devoted family, the Duplays, with whom he boarded. In the end, he stopped coming even to meetings of the Committee of Public Safety.

Robespierre also had an intense, lifelong concern with his image and with his standing in the eyes of others. His obsessive focus on his physical appearance—the powdered hair and impeccably groomed outfits—is well known. His room at the Duplays was filled with various likenesses of himself—paintings, engravings, a bust, and a bas-relief. From his youth, when he entered essay contests, Robespierre strove not just to excel, but to rise above his fellows. He fed off the applause he received whenever he spoke at the Convention, and preferred the company of his admirers to that of his peers. He seemed to revel not just in being virtuous for virtue's sake, but in being more virtuous than his fellows. And when it seemed that others, such as Danton, were surpassing him, he struck back with vengeance.

Those who have found little good in the man point to Robespierre's advocacy of the guillotine as the clearest proof of his hypocrisy. Robespierre never once attended an execution; he was too sickened by the sight of blood. How, they argue, could anyone who admitted to being unnerved by seeing human misery, yet who authorized the mass slaughter of thousands, be sincere about loving the people?

The Final Enigma

Should Robespierre finally be condemned? Perhaps the answer may never be finally decided. Shortly before he was led to his death, Robespierre had asked his captors for a pen and paper (he had a wounded jaw, which made speech too painful). His request was denied. Students of history will forever wonder what Robespierre would have written had he been given that last chance. Would it have been a final confession or apology, born of the pain of experiencing the methods of the Terror firsthand? Or would it simply have been a last striking out at his enemies? Robespierre carried the final key to his soul to his grave.

These contrasts of appearance, manner, and habits merely point to more fundamental differences. Danton, with his superabundance of energy, was a man who loved life and enjoyed his fellow men and women as individuals. Robespierre lived apart from other people, and his concern was for ideas and ideals and for humanity in the abstract. Danton can serve as a fitting symbol for the year when the people—the sans-culottes—finally came into their own. Robespierre personifies the final stage of the Revolution, when the obsession to mold the nation into an abstract vision of the ideal state became so overpowering that anything, even human life, would be sacrificed to achieve the goal.

Danton was removed from the Committee of Public Safety largely because of his efforts to achieve peace with France's enemies through negotiation. The recent string of defeats angered citizens and made them much less tolerant of any compromise with those hostile to the Revolution.

Charlotte Corday

Then, in mid-July, the activities of a young girl from the provinces led to still less tolerance. Charlotte Corday was an idealistic young woman from Normandy who had been strongly influenced by the deposed Girondins and their sympathizers. She became convinced that many of the evils that beset her country were due to the fall of the Girondins. And the Girondins' fall, she believed, was the working of Jean-Paul Marat. On July 13 Charlotte Corday knocked at the door of 30 Rue des Cordeliers and asked permission to see the principal resident, Jean-Paul Marat. Persistence gained her admittance to the room where the editor of *The Friend of the People* was soaking in a high copper tub. They exchanged a few words about the political scene in Normandy, the province from which they both hailed. Then Charlotte coolly pulled a dinner knife out of her shirt and plunged it into Marat's chest. Her aim was good. Within minutes her victim was dead.

News of Marat's death alarmed the entire nation. In the eyes of many working people Marat was a hero, their champion. His assassination, they were convinced, was part of a larger plot to topple the Revolution. The people demanded that the new government deal more forcefully with treachery within France as well as without.

The government responded. For several weeks the newly formed Convention had been working on a new constitution for the nation. The delegates hoped that its strong democratic provisions would satisfy the people's demands for more radical action. This constitution granted the vote to all men, regardless of wealth or social status. (No other country in the world extended the vote to so many people. In the United States, for example, voters still had to meet a property requirement.) It also placed the responsibility for providing work and education on the shoulders of the government.

Later in the month the Convention took still more steps to satisfy the demands of the people. A decree was passed which would divide up the property of those who had fled into small plots even peasants could afford. A list of traitors and suspected traitors was drawn up, and by month's end the Committee of Public Safety was given the power to arrest them.

The men in power were becoming steadily more radical. A huge celebration marking the passage of the new constitution was planned for August 10. As delegates poured into Paris from all over the country, the new patriotic fervor reached a peak. Swept along on the tide of this swelling radicalism, the Convention took bold action to turn around the nation's dire military situation. On August 13 a *levée en masse*, or mass drafting, was called, the first such call-up in the history of the Western world. The language of the decree rang with stirring patriotism: "All citizens must discharge their debt to liberty. Some will give their labor, others their wealth, some their counsel, others their strength; all will give it the blood that flows in their veins." All unmarried men between the ages of eighteen and twenty-five were called to serve in the armed forces. But other citizens were to serve as well—married men were sent to armaments factories, women were asked to make clothes and tents and to serve in hospitals, and children tied bandages made from old linens. To further ensure the success of this massive attack on the enemies of the Revolution, it was decided that the Convention and its Committee of Public Safety would remain in power for the duration of the military crisis. The election of new representatives and other changes called for by the new Constitution would be postponed until the wartime emergency ended.

"We don't want promises—we want bread!":
Gains for the Hébertists

The government assumed that the *levée en masse* and other measures passed in July and August would satisfy the demand of most of the people for a more forceful and radical commitment to the Revolution. But it was mistaken. There were still citizens, primarily in Paris, for whom even this was not enough.

As the summer progressed the republican armies continued to fare badly. The *levée en masse* was not yielding enough men. On September 4

This contemporary engraving shows men signing up to join the army. The French Revolution transformed the nation's armed services. In addition to the great number of new soldiers brought in by the *levée en masse,* the opening of the officers' ranks to non nobles helped to make it truly a people's army. Many noble officers, unable to win the confidence of the men under them, or simply opposed to the Revolutionary government, left. This paved the way for a whole new generation of non noble army careerists. *Art Resource/ Lauros-Giraudon.*

republican forces surrendered the city of Toulon to the English. Once again the people were convinced that treason was to blame and that the Convention and Committee were not doing enough to stop it. On top of the military setback, Paris's supply of bread was once again reaching critically low levels. Action, many felt, was essential.

At this point a new leader of the city's most radical element came to the fore. For some time, Jacques-René Hébert had been regularly turning out his revolutionary journal, *Le Père Duchesne (Father Oak).* But this polite, soft-spoken man had far greater ambitions for himself.

In September, sensing the time was ripe, he had begun to organize the radical Parisians.

The day of the surrender of Toulon a spontaneous demonstration for bread and higher wages had begun outside the municipal head-quarters at the Hôtel de Ville. Although the Convention assured the crowd that the price of all basic foods would be regulated within the week, the demonstrators were not satisfied. "We don't want promises," they cried, "we want bread, and we want it now."

The day following, a huge mass of workingmen and -women, in large part organized by Hébert, marched from the Hôtel de Ville to the Manège where the Convention was meeting. They swarmed into the assembly hall carrying placards reading "War on aristocrats!" and "War on tyrants!" This time they demanded not just bread, but also price controls, the speedy arrest and trial of suspected traitors, and a revolutionary army to enforce such measures. "No more mercy for traitors," cried one. "Let *terreur* [terror] be the order of the day," declared others.

In the weeks that followed, the Convention passed the measures the radical Hébertists called for, and more as well. Maximum prices were set on basic commodities. A revolutionary army was created. The number of judges and prosecutors working for the Revolutionary Tribunal, the court set up to try suspected enemies of the Revolution, was increased. A Law of Suspects was passed, establishing standards for determining political disloyalty and calling for the arrest of all who met them. (These criteria were very broad; a person could be accused on the basis of his "conduct . . . connections . . . remarks, or . . . writings.") The machinery for a complete transformation of the nation was being set in place. All that was needed now was a central government powerful enough to set it and keep it in motion.

By the end of September that need had been met. The national government had been transformed into a streamlined and efficient war machine, centered in the body of twelve men who formed the Committee of Public Safety.

"Terror shall be the order of the day"

The twelve who made up the Committee were a relatively undistinguished group. Most of them were provincial, middle-class lawyers; only one, the actor Collot d'Herbois, might be called a man of the people. Billaud-Varenne had been a drifter, Herault de Sechelles had a reputation as a connoisseur, and Saint-Just, barely out of his youth, was known as a playboy. Saint-André was a Protestant minister. Although they were a well-educated group, they had very little experience in practical government. Yet these twelve men now had the power to run the country. Local surveillance committees had to send them reports of their proceedings. "Representatives on mission" were appointed to go out to the provinces to see that government policies were carried out. And over the next ten months these twelve men were to transform France.

The Committee met daily in a room in the Tuileries Palace. Their meetings were conducted informally around a large, oval table strewn with piles of papers. They kept no minutes, had no agendas. Frequently debate went on late into the night. The twelve men were never all present at the same time, as they took turns joining their representatives on mission in the provinces to oversee the shaping of the Revolution. The amount of work they undertook was immense.

De-Christianization

Today students studying the French Revolution learn that the Convention voted to abolish monarchy and founded the First Republic on September 22, 1793. Back then, however, the day was referred to as 1 Vendémiaire, in the Year I. France was on the threshold of a new era, and the Committee wanted a completely new calendar, one that began numbering years from the date the monarchy was done away with and that created all new months, weeks, and days.

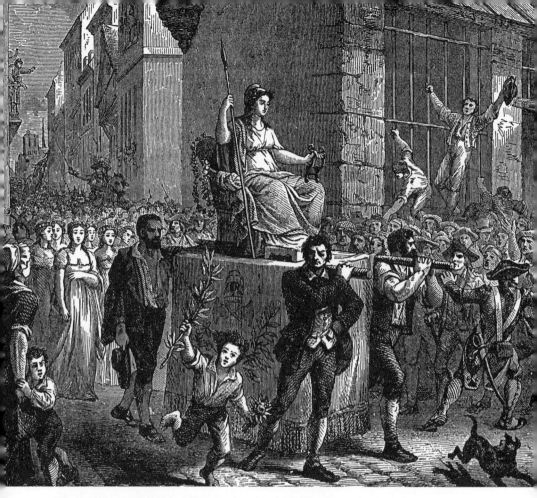

The goddess of Reason (played often by a local young woman) replaced the Virgin Mary in processions through the streets of French cities. The faith in human reason, which had begun during the Enlightenment, grew to great proportions during the years of the Revolution. In November 1793 even Paris's famed Notre Dame Cathedral was host to a Festival of Reason. *Culver Pictures, Inc.*

The new revolutionary calendar was, most noticeably, not based on Christianity. Time was no longer counted from the year of Jesus's birth. New ten-day weeks completely did away with Sundays.

The new calendar was the spearhead of a growing movement of de-Christianization. As the nation embarked on its new, most radical phase, people believed that Christianity had to be done away with and replaced by devotion to the state. For some time people had already been turning away from the Church. Many had ceased going to Mass. Places named after saints had been given new, revolutionary titles. But in September 1793 this trend became a movement.

It began in the provincial city of Nevers, where the local representative on mission spoke against what he called the trickery and deception of religion and against the celibacy of priests. He ordered all priests to marry or to adopt a child or to support an elderly person. He had priestly vestments burned and religious images destroyed. Valuable religious articles and ornaments were turned over to the national treasury. Religious services outside churches were banned.

Setting the Scene:
The Revolutionary Calendar

If anthropologists, working hundreds or thousands of years from now, were to try to describe our culture, they would deduce much from an analysis of our calendar. They would probably conclude that the Christian churches were central to us, since the way we number our years has its origin in the date of Jesus' birth and since Sunday, the day traditionally set aside for Christian worship, appears as the first day of the week. They might also conclude that we are not a very rational people, looking at the four months with thirty days, the seven months with thirty-one, and February with twenty-eight. Unable to find any reasonable explanation for this odd setup, they might decide that it was maintained simply because we had a deep respect for tradition.

Most of us probably don't stop to think about what our calendar says about us. The French revolutionaries, however, did. They were convinced that the creation of the First Republic in 1792 was the most important event in the history of mankind. They believed that it marked the beginning of a new era, one that would be characterized by rationality rather than by superstitious religion and blind allegiance to tradition. They wanted their calendar to reflect all these things and to help people to make the break with the past complete.

So, on October 5, 1793, a new calendar and timekeeping system were officially put into effect. To show the central importance of the Revolution, years were to be counted from the founding of the Republic. Thus from September 22, 1792, to September 22, 1793, would be the Year I, the following year the Year II, etc. As a demonstration of the revolutionaries' dedication to the principle of reason, they would do away with the old, arbitrary divisions of days and time. Instead, each year would be divided into twelve months of thirty days each, and each month into three "weeks," called *decades,* of ten days each. The days were identified rationally, by number; for example, *quintidi* for the fifth day, *decadi* for the tenth. This would leave five days over at the end of the year. These would be special festival days, to be called *sans-culottides.* An overhauling of the timekeeping system was even decreed (although it never caught on). Each day was to be divided into ten parts, and each of these broken down again into tenths.

In the naming of their new months and days, the revolutionaries revealed even more of what they considered important. The months were named for such natural events or conditions as "fog" or "harvest." In addition to its marking as *quintidi* or *decadi,* every day of the year was dedicated to a different "treasure of rural life"—a plant, animal, or farm tool. Thus a typical week might consist of Snowday, Iceday, Honeyday, Waxday, Dogday, Strawday, Petroleumday, Coalday, Resinday, and Flailday. The five *sans-culottides* festivals were dedicated to some of the principles the revolutionaries held dearest: Virtue, Genius, Labor,

Opinion, and Rewards, in that order. (On the Festival of Opinion, all citizens would be invited to speak their minds about public officials; it was to be a day of lampoons and caricatures.)

For the next fifteen years, people spoke of the 9 Thermidor, of the decrees of Ventôse, of the Year II or the Year X. It was not until Napoleon was crowned emperor of France in 1804 that the country agreed to return to the old Gregorian calendar.

The Months of the Revolutionary Calendar

Vendémiaire	the month of the grape harvest	September 22–October 21
Brumaire	the month of fog	October 22–November 20
Frimaire	the month of frost	November 21–December 20
Nivôse	the month of snow	December 21–January 19
Pluviôse	the month of rain	January 20–February 18
Ventôse	the month of wind	February 19–March 20
Germinal	the month of sowing	March 21–April 19
Floréal	the month of flowers	April 20–May 19
Prairial	the month of meadows	May 20–June 18
Messidor	the month of harvest	June 19–July 18
Thermidor	the month of heat	July 19–August 17
Fructidor	the month of fruit	August 18–September 16
Sans-culottides		September 17–21

It was not long before similar measures were being enacted back in Paris. On November 11 a ceremony celebrating Reason was staged in Notre Dame Cathedral. Soldiers paraded busts of revolutionary heroes through the aisles. Days later the Commune ordered all churches in the city closed.

From Paris de-Christianization quickly spread across the nation. In most of the major towns cathedrals were stripped of their valuables and converted into "temples of Reason." Many other churches were simply closed. Many priests resigned their offices and married. Non-Christian, revolutionary names for babies became popular. In at least one village they totaled more than two thirds of all names bestowed on new infants. Indeed, the new government's aim of replacing religion with a worshipful devotion to the state appeared to be succeeding.

Revolutionary Justice

The suppression of Christianity was just one sign of change under the First Republic. De-Christianization accompanied the infamous period of new, "revolutionary" justice known as the Terror.

You have no more grounds for restraint against the enemies of the new order, and liberty must prevail at any price. . . You must punish not merely traitors but the indifferent as well; you must punish whoever is passive in the Republic. . . . We must rule by iron those who cannot be ruled by justice.

These words, sure to inspire fear in all who heard them, were spoken by Saint-Just, the same man who just the preceding June had made an appeal for moderation. Nor was Saint-Just alone in his about-face. "Softness to traitors will destroy us all," declared Robespierre. By the end of September the Committee of Public Safety came down whole-heartedly for the new harsh policy.

On the morning of October 16 Henri Sanson entered the cell of Marie Antoinette, tied her hands behind her back, and proceeded to cut off her hair. Her face was pale, her eyes ringed with circles of weariness. With her newly shorn head she scarcely looked like a queen. Her composure, however, was that of a sovereign. Throughout her journey to the guillotine, she held her head stiffly and stared straight ahead. Her only words were an apology to the executioner—for having stepped on his foot while mounting the scaffold. In an instant she had joined her husband in his miserable end.

The death of the Queen began a steady stream of "traitors" to the Place de la Revolution. And while Marie Antoinette had long been considered a villain in the people's eyes, this was not true of many of those who followed her. Many of the October victims had once been considered friends of the Revolution. The twenty Girondins who went to the blade had only months prior been among the radicals in the government. In November Madame Roland shared their fate. She was followed several days later by Jean Sylvain Bailly, the former mayor of Paris, and the man before whom the revolutionaries had sworn the famous Tennis Court Oath.

Nor were sentences to the guillotine limited to prominent political figures. As the fall progressed, dozens of obscure men and women lost their lives as well. In fact, the guillotine proved a grimly democratic instrument. The blood of nobles and peasants, nuns and atheists, men and women mingled beneath its blade. Although the upper classes might once have been considered the chief enemies of the Revolution, over three quarters of those executed were members of the third estate.

The charges brought against the victims were as varied as their backgrounds. Generals were condemned for defeats on the battlefield. Publishers died for printing counterrevolutionary writings. Some, simply on the testimony of jealous neighbors, were found guilty of "depraving public morals." Others went to their deaths because they were related to a convicted traitor; sometimes whole families were sent to the blade.

This gruesome spectacle was not confined to Paris; only 16 percent of the guillotinings of the Revolution took place in the capital. In some of the provinces the butchery was even worse, as the provincials sometimes resorted to still more frightening means of execution. In Lyons, known as a center of counterrevolutionary activity, the local representative of the Terror government had several hundred victims lined up and blasted by cannon when he became impatient with the pace of the guillotine. In Nantes, two thousand of the convicted were towed into the middle of the Loire river on barges, which were then sunk.

And throughout France the trip to the guillotine was often only the culmination of weeks or months of torturous imprisonment. Since no place was equipped to handle the swollen numbers of prisoners, gross overcrowding was the norm. Sometimes twenty or even thirty suspects were locked up in a single small, windowless room. Malnutrition and disease were rampant, and thousands died before they reached the guillotine—or even came to trial.

"Economy in human blood":
The Short-lived Movement for Moderation

Throughout the fall Hébert and his followers had been actively promoting the policy of extreme terror, as well as taking the lead in the de-Christianization movement. By December, however, people began to react. Some of the members of the Committee of Public Safety became uneasy about such extremism, especially about extreme de-Christianization. They feared the assault on the Church might discredit the Revolution in the eyes of some of its supporters. They were also alarmed at the extent of independent power wielded by the representatives on mission who were overseeing these radical measures.

Robespierre, always more paranoid than the rest, suspected a foreign plot. He was convinced that foreign spies were attempting to set one member of the Committee against another and were trying to arouse public opinion against the Revolution through such policies as radical de-Christianization and excessive executions. In late November the Committee began to take action.

". . . [W]e have no other fanaticism to fear than that of immoral men, paid by foreign courts to reawaken fanaticism and give our

Revolution an appearance of immorality," Robespierre declared in an address to the Assembly. Foreign courts, he continued, maintained an "army of spies . . . in the heart of the popular societies."

Robespierre headed a movement to increase the Committee's control over its far-flung representatives on mission. On December 4, 1793, a decree was passed that effectively concentrated all power in the central government. Robespierre also spoke out strongly against the de-Christianizers. Attacks on the Church were ordered stopped.

Throughout the fall Georges Danton had been absent from Paris. No longer a member of the Committee, he had retired to his family farm in Arcis-sur-Aube, about a hundred miles east of Paris. When he returned in mid-November, he was pleased to find a less radical mood prevailing among the nation's leaders. He himself had been repulsed by the mass executions of the fall—and had shed tears over the deaths of the Girondins. So now he threw his vast energies into the attack on the radical Hébertists. "Perhaps the Terror once served a useful purpose, but it should not hurt innocent people," he declared. What the nation needed was "economy in human blood."

Others among the deputies were quick to rally around Danton's strong leadership. Camille Desmoulins, an old friend of Danton, began publication of a new journal, *The Old Gray Friar*. Its pages were devoted to attacks on the radicals and, eventually, to attacks upon the Terror itself. For a while it seemed the movement for relaxation of the Terror might triumph. Robespierre seemed sympathetic to it. He had approved the first two issues of *Le Vieux Cordelier* and in mid-December even supported the creation of a new "Committee of Clemency," whose job would be to review lists of suspects and remove from them any who were innocent. A number of the radical Hébertists were arrested and thrown in jail.

But Robespierre had great difficulty truly trusting anyone, and by late December he had begun to suspect the Dantonists of treason as well. He was unnerved by later issues of *The Old Friar*, which went beyond an attack on the Hébertists to an attack on the Terror. In addition, evidence was mounting that one of the prominent Dantonists was indeed involved in a corrupt money-making scheme involving a foreign company—the "foreign plot" Robespierre had warned against.

The Committee's openness to the moderate Dantonist faction came to an abrupt halt. The Committee of Clemency was disbanded. Robespierre denounced Desmoulins' journal and demanded that it be burned. To the leader of the Committee and his supporters, all factions, whether radical or conservative, were henceforth to be considered equally dangerous.

During the first months of 1794 the Committee of Public Safety asserted over and over that all critics were dangerous agents of a counterrevolutionary plot. It was only a matter of time before the verbal attack took a more violent form.

"Let conspirators of all kinds tremble": The Purging of the Hébertists and Dantonists

---

The Hébertists were the first to go. In March the radical members of the Cordeliers Club planned a demonstration to protest a recent food shortage. When word of this got out, the Committee of Public Safety used it as an excuse to have all the leading Hébertists arrested. Their trials were a mere formality. Before the month's end, Hébert and seventeen of his followers had gone to the guillotine. It would not be long before the moderates would follow.

Members of the Committee of Public Safety began to step up their accusations of Danton. Still, the blustering lawyer could not believe his longtime companion Robespierre would actually take action against him. Late in March the two men happened to meet at a dinner party. "Let us forget our private resentments, and think only of the country, its needs and dangers," Danton said to his fellow revolutionary. "Liberty cannot be secured unless criminals lose their heads," was Robespierre's eventual answer.

Despite this merciless reply, Robespierre was actually reluctant to have Danton arrested. But fellow members of the Committee eventually persuaded him that this was an essential step. To prosecute the moderates while sparing their leader would not be possible, they argued. The warrant was signed early on the morning on the last day of March.

Danton had given up any thoughts of a physical fight for his life. But so long as breath still filled his powerful lungs, he would not surrender his right to fight verbally.

When the trial opened on April 2, Danton burst into the courtroom like an enraged bull. Soon his booming voice so filled the room that, it was said, it could be heard on the opposite bank of the Seine. Again and again the president of the Assembly rang his bell for the speaker to be silent, but to no avail. "A man who is fighting for his life pays no attention to bells," Danton retorted, and on he went, tearing into what he termed the "present dictatorship." He refused to be seated until promised he could continue his testimony the following day.

The prosecutor knew that if the second day of the trial were a repeat of the first, the jury might be very likely to turn in a verdict of "not guilty." Unsure of how to act, he contacted the Committee of Public Safety. Saint-Just produced a decree stating that any accused person who insulted the court should be forbidden to plead in his own defense. "Murderers!" Danton cried out. But he knew then that his fate was sealed. No standard of justice would be allowed to stand in the way of the verdict the Committee was after. He left his prosecutors, however, with an ominous warning: "The people will tear my enemies to pieces within three months," he declared.

The next day, proceedings were begun an hour and a half earlier than usual. That way the galleries would be largely empty of spectators likely to be sympathetic to the accused. The trial concluded hastily, with the jury returning the sought-after verdict, and by afternoon Danton was jostling in a red cart on his way to the guillotine.

Danton stood tall and strong as he awaited the call to the platform.

"Above all, don't forget to show my head to the people," he remarked to the executioner. "It's well worth having a look at."

A Republic of Virtue

One woman was thrown into a tizzy over a decision of what to serve at a dinner for members of her section. She was sure some of the guests would be insulted if she served a "dish of the people," such as beans. On the other hand, she feared the accusation of being too high class if she served something as fancy as pheasant. Another woman, who owned a dress shop, provided tricolor cockades for the young women who worked for her to wear when they went out into the street. She hoped that might quiet any suspicions that her girls were not proper revolutionaries. In the theaters, plays were censored to make sure audiences were not corrupted by unrevolutionary lines. By June 1794 regulation and fear governed much of a person's day.

With the deaths of Marat and Danton, the one a favorite journalist and the other a beloved leader, many people also began to lose their faith in the Revolution.

The Committee of Public Safety was aware that the people were growing apathetic. What was needed, Robespierre and his followers believed, was an intensified effort at transforming France into the "republic of virtue" about which he had so long dreamed.

Ten days after the death of Danton, Saint-Just had addressed the nation. The subject of his speech was public morale. ". . . Revolutionary government does not mean war or conquest, but the transition from evil to good," he proclaimed. It was the duty of the government, Saint-Just believed, "to transform men into what [it] wants them to be." For some time the revolutionaries had been attempting to create institutions that would foster "virtue" in people. Just what did they mean by "virtue"?

Most importantly, virtue referred to civic-mindedness. The revolutionaries dreamed of a nation whose every citizen took a natural, unselfish interest in the good of the country as a whole. But they also understood virtue in its more usual sense—as referring to lives marked by frugality in spending, respect for property, and modesty in dress and manner.

Efforts to create a "republic of virtue" had been under way for some time. Robespierre believed strongly that such a state would have to be firmly grounded in the principle of equality. Furthermore, he believed that the creation of equality would require the elimination of poverty. Prices and wages were already regulated by the government. In February the Committee of Public Safety passed decrees, called the "Laws of Ventôse," intended to provide further relief from poverty by confiscating the property of anyone found guilty by the revolutionary tribunals and distributing it to the poor. These laws were never systematically carried out, and so had little effect on the lives of the nation's workers and peasants. Nevertheless, the idea they represented—that the government had control over the distribution of private property—was radical in the extreme, a forerunner of the doctrine of socialism.

That same month the Convention gave even greater evidence of the radical nature of its commitment to equality: It enacted legislation that granted freedom to French slaves—nearly seventy years before the American Emancipation Proclamation!

In December the government had taken over control of education and made three years of education compulsory and free to all. Then, in May, it proposed the opening of a teacher-training college. This would make the government even better able "to teach republican laws and morality." In addition, it would give the government more control over the family, ties to which it viewed as a dangerous rival to national loyalty.

Plans were also made to reform the French language, ridding it of its many different regional variations (blocks to national unity) and of all coarse expressions. Artists and writers were told to "inject republican morality into works intended for public instruction." There was even an attempt to design a new national costume, intended to exemplify and promote the new revolutionary consciousness of equality and modest virtue. Robespierre was shrewd enough, however, to know that institutions alone were not enough to bring about the kind of total transformation of spirit he dreamed. His vision could not be accomplished, he believed, without the cooperation of religion.

The Cult of the Supreme Bring

A bright June sun shone down on houses bedecked with garlands and oak branches. The streets were filled with men in red caps and women in white dresses with tricolor sashes. The crowd craned their necks, straining to see what was happening in front of the Tuileries Palace, where several strikingly ugly statues stood. At last a slight figure appeared, meticulously dressed in a brilliant blue coat and snappy buff trousers, a bouquet of flowers bound with a tricolor ribbon in his hands. He mounted the amphitheater and spoke—some might say droned on—for what seemed hours. Then he took a lighted torch and proceeded to set fire to the ugly statues. A whisper spread through the crowd that these were meant to represent selfishness, atheism, and discord. As the flames died down, a young woman dressed in the Grecian style—could she be "Wisdom"?—appeared on the structure where just minutes before the ugly statues had stood. The blue-coated figure again addressed the crowd. Then he led the deputies and the crowd out toward the Champ de Mars. There, on what had just a week earlier been level ground, a great hill rose up, topped by a noble-looking statue and a tall tree. Presently the newly constructed hill was surrounded by groups of people—deputies and regular citizens, young and old, men and women. Young girls strewing flower petals circulated among them. An orchestra began to play, and the crowds raised their hands as though to pay homage to someone or something. The festivities drew to a resounding conclusion with a round of artillery fire and cheers of "Long live the Republic!"

The Festival of the Supreme Being, which Robespierre orchestrated to launch his new religion of state, was a masterpiece of stagecraft. The small mound in the center of the vast crowds had been created just for the event. The many thousands who attended included the deputies of the Convention and all public officials. *Musée Carnavalet (Art Resource/Lauros-Giraudon).*

The massive festival was intended to honor the "Supreme Being." It was the brainchild of the man who had served as its blue-coated master of ceremonies—Maximilien Robespierre. Robespierre had long derided Catholicism for its useless superstition and priestly class. But he maintained a belief in God. What was needed, he concluded, was a new form of religion. Robespierre proposed a national cult of the Supreme Being. The new religion would have no priests, no dogmas save belief in God and in man's immortal soul. But it would have plenty of festivals to rally the nation's spirit. The festival celebrated in Paris on June 8 was to be the first of forty.

The Great Terror

"One rules the people by reason and its enemies by Terror," said Saint-Just. "Virtue without . . . terror is disastrous," said Robespierre. The stepped-up efforts to foster civic virtue in France's citizens was not the only tactic the Committee of Public Safety adopted in the aftermath of the purge of the Hébertists and Dantonists. Along with the efforts to shape a new consciousness of virtue among the nation's citizens came new measures designed to root out and eliminate all traitors.

In June the Committee of Public Safety passed a decree that greatly expanded the numbers of people who could be considered "public enemies" and, thus, be brought to trial. It also greatly reduced the means of defense allowed a suspect. Legal counsel would no longer be admitted, and witnesses would not be allowed except in very special cases. Finally, it forbade the revolutionary tribunals to apply any penalty other than death to those found guilty.

The passage of this "Law of 22 Prairial" stepped up the pace of trials and executions to a fevered pitch. From June 22 to the end of July the number of executions in Paris totaled over thirteen hundred— more than the number put to death in the fifteen previous months. Some of this great leap in numbers can be explained by the Committee's effort to concentrate the work of the revolutionary tribunals in Paris. But in the main it represents a sheer increase in harsh revolutionary "justice." Sentences of "guilty" were issued on the basis of mere rumor. One judge, impatient with one of his colleagues for taking time to hear evidence, complained, "He has to have proofs, like the ordinary courts of the *ancien régime.*" If a judge felt the judicial process was proceeding too slowly, he tried prisoners collectively and issued

Scenes in the prisons of the Revolution could be as agonizing as those at the foot of the guillotine. Here, in a close-up from a painting by C. L. Muller, prisoners wait anxiously as a guard prepares to read the day's list of guillotine victims. *Alinari/Art Resource.*

a joint sentence. The prosecutor in Paris made boasts about how many hundreds he would be able to "take the tops off" in a week.

By July fear ruled the nation. Men, women, and children went to bed at night dreading a knock at the door. Few dared speak openly, for fear that a casual remark might be used as evidence of lack of proper revolutionary spirit. When, how, was it all to end?

The Fall of Robespierre

The mumbling had begun around the time of the festival of the Supreme Being. "Just listen to the pontiff!" whispered one deputy, annoyed at the length of Robespierre's speech. "Tyrant," said another. "The [fellow] isn't satisfied with being the boss; he's got to be God as well," grumbled a sans-culotte.

Dissatisfaction with the path the revolutionary government was taking, and in particular with the man who more and more clearly had emerged as its leader, mounted along with the death toll. And, in a departure from the last ten months, the dissatisfaction began to invade the Committee of Public Safety itself. Since the previous September the Committee had been a model of political unity. But, worn down by weeks of late nights and never-ending work, on edge because of the summer heat, its members began to complain about one another. In the main their hostility focused on Robespierre. Never one to socialize, Robespierre now isolated himself even more. Toward the end of June he stopped coming to meetings of the Committee. There were grumblings that he was becoming a dictator and that he would turn against even his closest colleagues to achieve that end. As the summer heated up, so did tensions within the Committee.

The Reign of Terror had originally been instituted in the face of a desperate military situation. Its aim was to rally the nation and enable it to defend itself against its enemies. By late June, however, that reason for being had nearly evaporated. In April, French troops had entered Sardinia; in May, Spain; and in June, the Netherlands, where a decisive victory at Fleurus paved the way to making the republican armies masters of Belgium. Not only had France recaptured much of the territory it had lost; it had gained new territory as well.

The military victories led to increased boldness on the part of many deputies, who saw little reason to keep on with the Terror. As the number of executions mounted, it seemed only a matter of time before the Convention erupted.

It was Robespierre, however, who struck first. An astute man, the bewigged deputy was keenly aware of the growing opposition. On July 26, dressed in the same stunning blue coat he had worn for the Festival of the Supreme Being, he marched into the Convention and approached the rostrum. He spoke for over two hours, accusing the deputies of all manner of disloyalty to the nation and to himself, and promising to "purify" the Committee of Public Safety of all such influences.

Normally, Robespierre's speeches were greeted with resounding applause. At first this occasion seemed to follow the expected pattern. But then the Superintendent of Finance, Pierre Joseph Cambon, rose from his seat. "It is time to tell the whole truth," he announced to the suddenly quieted audience. "One man alone is paralyzing the will of the National Convention. *And that man is Robespierre.*"

Within minutes others rushed from their seats to support Cambon. In no time the Convention erupted into a swirl of noisy arguments. By closing it was clear Robespierre was doomed.

The next day, after several deputies made even more pointed attacks on him, Robespierre attempted to reply. But his words were drowned out by cries of "Down with the tyrant!" and "To the guillotine!" At one point Robespierre lost his voice altogether. "Ah, Danton's blood chokes you," someone chided him. By the time his arrest had been proposed and voted on, Robespierre was slumped in a seat, exhausted. His two chief supporters on the Committee of Public Safety, Saint-Just and Couthon, were also placed under arrest.

When news of the arrest reached the Paris Commune, this group, always more radical than the Convention, decided to protest and to throw their support behind Robespierre. But mustering support for him among the people proved more difficult than it had in the past. Despite their history of radicalism, Parisians were weary of the endless executions and of the revolutionaries' repeated failures to improve the workers' standard of living. The Commune managed to free Robespierre and his colleagues but, without the support of the people of Paris, knew they could not protect them.

The night of July 27 was the turning point. At seven in the evening, City Hall, where the Robespierrists were being quartered, was surrounded by thirty-four hundred soldiers loyal to him. But as the evening wore on, the men thought more carefully about where their loyalties now lay. By one fifteen in the morning, only two hundred of the soldiers remained. In the early hours of July 28, the Robespierrists were easily overwhelmed by the forces of the Convention.

Early that evening the familiar sight of the carts of the condemned could once again be seen making their way through the city streets. This time, the crowds lining the way were unusually thick and unruly. "Down with the tyrant!" they called out over and over.

By seven thirty the head of the man who had himself been responsible for the heads of hundreds was tossed into the blood-soaked basket.

CHAPTER

6

Chronology

Year II	1794	
Thermidor	end of July–early August	"Thermidorean Reaction"—powers of Committee of Public Safety and Paris sections reduced prisoners released
Year III		
	fall	"gilded youth" assault revolutionaries and their institutions

•

	1795	
12 Germinal and 1 Prairial	April 1 and May 20	sans-culotte revolts in Paris, the second silenced by National Guard
Prairial	May–June	White Terror: conservative reprisals in provinces
20 Prairial	June 8	Count of Provence declares himself Louis XVIII
6–9 Messidor	June 24–27	royalist attack
5 Fructidor	August 22	Constitution of Year III passed

Year IV

Vendémiaire	September	"decree of two thirds" requires two thirds of delegates to new government to come from Convention
13 Vendémiaire	October 5	protest against decree of two thirds silenced by Napoleon
4 Brumaire	October 26	Directory assumes power

•

1796

	spring	conspiracy by the radical Babeuf
		Napoleon begins Italian campaign (through 1797, years V and VI)

•

Year VII   **1798**   Napoleon begins Egyptian campaign

•

Year VIII   **1799**

18–19 Brumaire	November 9–10	Napoleon leads coup against Directory and becomes First Consul

Elegant society life made a strong comeback in the years following the end of the Terror. This engraving shows Parisians at the Café Frascati, in the time of Napoleon. After the Revolution, France's economy began to revive and many new fortunes were made. The newly rich enjoyed displaying their wealth. *Art Resource/Lauros-Giraudon.*

Chapter Six:

The Fate of the Revolution

Gone were the simple, modest styles of Jacobin days. Instead, men dressed in tight trousers, coats flared to an extreme, and dramatic oversized cravats (neck scarves). At their sides were stylish women, whose fashionable dresses were so flimsy and low cut that it seemed as though they were wearing nothing at all. Their wigs, although Grecian in style rather than piled high, had curls as elaborate as any coiffures of the *ancien régime.*

Every evening these flashily dressed men and women could be seen speeding off somewhere in fancy carriages painted with intricate designs. No longer was it a political meeting or a section dinner to which they were traveling. Instead people made their way by the score to the capital's restaurants, theaters, gaming rooms, and dance halls. In fine restaurants customers ordered from luxurious menus, and meals cost the equivalent of two months' food for a worker's family. In gaming rooms men and women with newly made fortunes bet thousands on single hands of cards.

The theaters, closed for months, were once again open and immensely popular. They were crowded every night, not only on account of the newly revived comedies, but also for the activities of their back rooms. These were described in one police report of the time as "sewers of debauchery and vice."

And dancing had become all the rage, with new dance halls opening weekly. At some dances, called *bals des victimes,* guests sported thin, red silk bands around their necks—reminders of the heyday of the guillotine. Salons had also been revived. Lacking much of the charm of earlier years, however, they were now principally places to see and be seen.

Did Robespierre's death end the Revolution? That question has been answered in various ways, depending on how the Revolution is defined. Yet certainly something had changed in the months following 9 Thermidor (July 17). Indeed, the whole face and character of life in Paris seemed to have changed. A transformation of style and attitude had taken place, and it pointed to deeper shifts in the mode of the country.

A New Conservatism

The change did not occur overnight. In the weeks after the ousting of Robespierre, most of the principal revolutionary institutions—the Committee of Public Safety, the Revolutionary Tribunal, the Convention, and the Constitution—continued in place. The Jacobin Club was reopened on 11 Thermidor (July 29). However, from the day Robespierre and his followers went to the guillotine, the forces of reaction began to grow in strength. It was not long before a new conservatism had made its presence felt in the nation's political structures, and put an abrupt end to the brief reign of the nation's working people.

This was first evident in the government of the capital itself. The Paris Commune immediately had been abolished, and over seventy of its members sent to the guillotine for having been supportive of the Robespierrists. Not long afterward, the powers of the sections were reduced, their meeting times shifted to midday so as to exclude workingmen.

Although executions continued, a great cry of the people for a new leniency went up and was soon answered. The Law of Prairial, which had deprived accused persons of legal defense and made almost any-thing grounds for conviction, was repealed. The prisons of Paris let loose hundreds of those who had been awaiting trial or punishment. In one five-day period, over four hundred fifty men and women were set free. The Revolutionary Tribunal was reorganized, and the new Tribunal acquitted almost twenty times as many as it had during the Terror.

The Committee of Public Safety was also overhauled, its powers greatly reduced. And, in one of the most significant changes of this "Thermidorean reaction," as it is called (named after the month on the revolutionary calendar in which it took place), the governmental controls on wages and prices were lifted.

The Violence Continues

But the Revolution had set in motion an energy it was next to im-possible to control. Throughout the Revolution that energy had taken the form of violence, and the events of Thermidor were far from putting an end to that. The violence that just weeks before had been concentrated on counterrevolutionaries was now turned on the ter-rorists themselves.

All over Paris the streets began to swarm with actors, clerks, and other young men of the bourgeoisie, whose fastidious grooming, care-fully tended long locks, and exaggeratedly fashionable style of dressing made clear their lack of sympathy with the working class. Normally such a sight would be anything but threatening. However, these "gilded youth," as they were called, were armed with sticks weighted with lead at the end, and despite their dandyish good looks they proved as terrifying as any band of young toughs. They sacked busts and statues of revolutionary heroes, smashed the windows in the Jacobin Club, and attacked known Jacobins and other leftists.

In some sections of the country, there was little sense of vengeance toward those viewed as responsible for the Terror. In other places,

The modishly dressed young bourgeois men known as "gilded youth" used violence to crush any remaining traces of radical democracy. When the government decreed that the remains of Jean-Paul Marat should be kept in the Pantheon (an important civic building), "gilded youth" all over Paris smashed busts of Marat and threw them in the gutter. The Jacobin Club, shown here in the background, was eventually closed as a result of raids by these young men. *Culver Pictures, Inc.*

however, the violence was as severe as anything the Terror produced.

In the southeast regions of France the violence directed against terrorists was so severe it eventually constituted a "reign of terror" all its own. During this "White Terror"—so called because white was the color of the royal family—men organized themselves into lynch mobs with such names as "The Company of the Sun" and "The Company of Jesus." The Whites, often prompted by old personal, family, or local grievances as much as by hatred of the Revolution, gathered in taverns to plot and scheme secret assaults on their enemies. These plans were often carried out with the help of professional outlaws or assassins. In Provence and surrounding areas the White Terror made the early summer of 1795 a terrifying time for many.

Meanwhile, the sans-culottes had not yet completely given up on the use of violent tactics to achieve their ends, either. Certainly the new, more moderate government was not sympathetic to their cause. Not only had their ability to participate in sectional politics been virtually annihilated. In addition new regulations prohibited petition-ing and the meetings of public societies. But it was finally the winter of 1794–95 that moved Paris's working class to resort to whatever means they could use to make themselves heard.

The winter following Robespierre's demise was one of the worst in many years. For more than forty consecutive days, temperatures were freezing or below. Rivers froze. Fuel supplies were exhausted. Starving wolves roamed city streets, scavenging for food. Transporting what little food there was proved extremely difficult, and it was not long before the population of Paris was on the point of starvation. The government tried to distribute rice, but many lacked the fuel needed to cook it. Now that the limits on food prices had been lifted, the prices of basic items soared. Flour rose to a hundred times more than it had cost in 1790. By spring many had died from starvation, others from sheer desperation: The city's suicide rate that winter and spring rose dramatically.

On April 1 the people once again revolted. Crying out for "Bread!"

and "The Constitution of '93!" huge crowds, including many women and children, invaded the Convention. Although quickly subdued by members of the more well-to-do sections of the city, they were not quieted for good. Seven weeks later, on May 20, crowds once again marched on the Convention. This time the demonstrators were more insistent. In response, the government called out the National Guard. The Guard carried the day. Three days and many casualties later, the popular movement was completely silenced. The Convention outlawed the use of the term "revolutionary," officially reopened the churches, and terminated the Constitution of 1793.

The *Jeu de Bascule* (Seesaw Game)

Once set in motion, a pendulum swings back and forth for quite a long while before finally coming to rest. In a similar fashion, the forces set loose by the Revolution swung back and forth between conservative and leftist offensives and reactions for years after the Revolution had supposedly ended.

The last gasp of the Parisian sans-culottes in the spring of 1795 was followed several months later by an ultraconservative attempt at a royalist restoration. After the death of Louis XVI's son in prison, the former King's brother, the Count of Provence, declared himself Louis XVIII (Louis XVII to royalists who did not acknowledge the abolition of the monarchy). Inspired by the government's harsh repression of the sans-culottes, he concluded that the country might be ready for a return to monarchy and began to plot for a restoration of the old, divine-right kingship. The moderates in power had retreated sufficiently from their recent revolutionary stance to be open to the idea of a constitutional monarchy. But a complete reversion to the *ancien régime* was unthinkable. When émigré troops landed at Quiberon Bay in northwest France, General Hoche put a quick end to the royalists' scheme. More than seven hundred of the invading troops were shot for high treason.

Members of the Convention, which by this time was dominated by moderate delegates, were anxious to do what they could to guard against uprisings by either extreme. This concern for safeguarding citizens against possible working-class violence, while at the same time maintaining the rule of law that had been one of the basic, hard-won gains of the Revolution, provided much of the motivation for the drafting of a new constitution—the Constitution of the Year III.

"Equality consists in the fact that the law is the same for all." This statement, a far cry from the bold "men are born and remain free and equal in rights" of the Declaration of 1789, was typical of the shift in attitude embodied in the new constitution. Not only was equality proclaimed in much more modest tones; in addition, the right to rebellion was done away with, and a new right—the right to property—was added. The new Constitution made it clear that the real victors in the Revolution were principally the new men of property: the bourgeoisie. Voting rights for all men, for which Robespierre and the Jacobins had fought so valiantly, were abolished. In their place were the old property qualifications for voters and indirect election procedures of the Constitution of 1791.

The new Constitution also attempted to create checks and balances so that no one person or group could wield too much power. It set up a bicameral (two-chamber) legislature and put the executive power of the government in the hands of a group of five men called directors. Leadership of the group would rotate in order to prevent the consolidation of power in any one person's hands.

Despite the efforts of its drafters, the Constitution of the Year III failed to provide the rule of law it had been designed to bring about. Even before it had actually taken power, the Directory, as the new government was called, felt obliged to resort to force to maintain itself. The first test of its authority came when it asked the nation for approval of a decree that would require two thirds of the representatives elected to the new government to have been current members of the Convention. Many voters in Paris, frustrated by years of unmet demands at the hands of one regime after another, did not want those from the past to inherit the power in a new regime. In addition, royalists had become a strong faction in the capital, and they played upon the people's dissatisfaction. When the decree passed, Parisians turned out, twenty-five thousand strong, to protest it.

"A Whiff of Grapeshot"

The government had only four thousand troops in the capital. The outcome of the confrontation seemed clear. But the people had not counted on the new young commander from Corsica, Napoleon Bonaparte. The young man with the untidily combed black hair falling onto his shoulders was only twenty-six, but already something in him was desperate for a challenge. When asked if he would help lead the defense of the Convention, his "yes" was immediate. At once an innate instinct for military operations showed itself: "Where are the guns?" he asked.

The young commander lost no time in retrieving forty cannons from a camp outside Paris and positioning them strategically around the Tuileries. Over and over the rebels attempted to approach the Convention's headquarters, but they could not withstand the barrage of artillery fire with which they were greeted each time. By six in the evening, they had given up. Napoleon Bonaparte, with a "whiff of grapeshot," had quieted the royalists once and for all.

This uprising of Vendémiaire (October) set a precedent whose significance increased steadily in the years to come; only the army now had any real power to control the course of events in France. In the months since the fall of Robespierre, French forces had continued to win important victories against their enemies. Favorable peace terms had been concluded with Holland, Spain, and Prussia. Only with Austria and Great Britain was France still at war. The government of the Directory, on the other hand, was struggling to survive. It had begun with noble aims: to replace "the chaos which always accompanies revolutions by a new social order . . . wage vigorous war on royalists, revive patriotism, sternly suppress all factions, extinguish party spirit, destroy all desire for vengeance . . . revive industry and commerce, stamp out speculation, revitalize the arts and sciences, reestablish public credit and restore plenty."

Yet, from the outset, the new Directors and legislature fell sadly short of these lofty goals. They had inherited a bankrupt country in which inflation was rampant. When one Nantes housekeeper, trying to keep track of her household expenses, saw the price of bread rise to over fifty times its former rate, she gave up keeping records. Then, too, the nation was exhausted, tired of sacrifices for the common good. Citizens offered little support to the new government. Decadence and self-interest governed much of society life. Corruption among government officials was widespread. The daring of rural brigands and vagabonds had reached such heights that people feared traveling. Remarked one English visitor of the times: "Everyone plunges into the mud pool of vice as soon as he or she is strong enough to paddle in it without fear of parental or political control."

Once again, both royalists and Jacobins alternately began to protest the government's policies and actions. The next swing of the *jeu de bascule* was a radical Jacobin movement led by an obscure journalist, François Noël, who called himself Gracchus Babeuf. Babeuf demanded that the nation do away with private property altogether, insisting that land and property instead be held in common by the citizenry. Then, in the elections of 1797, it seemed the royalists were on the verge of taking over the country. The Directors responded to each threat with force. Babeuf and his supporters were executed. The election results of 1797 were invalidated, in direct defiance of the Constitution. Still, it seemed impossible for the moderates to secure the majority they needed in order to rule effectively. As the months rolled by, new military defeats further eroded the people's support of the government. By 1799 the authority of the Directors was at a low point.

Gracchus Babeuf, the revolutionary journalist who proposed that property be held in common and the crops grown on it distributed according to people's need, was a forerunner of nineteenth- and twentieth-century communists. Like many who followed in his footsteps, Babeuf believed his ideas could be implemented only with the help of violence. *Culver Pictures, Inc.*

What would it take to restore order and confidence to the embittered and embattled nation?

"Confidence from below, authority from above":
The Return to One-Man Rule

The Abbé Sieyès, the worldly priest who had aroused the common people in 1789 with his pamphlet *What Is the Third Estate?*, believed he had the answer. After ten years of experiments with self-rule, he concluded that the French people needed yet another new constitution and government—but one with a strong executive, or decision making, branch. His new formula for national well-being was "confidence from below, authority from above." Sieyès was by this time a shrewd politician. He knew that no such change could be achieved without the help of the military. He began to consider the nation's various generals.

Since his success in subduing the royalist uprising in Paris in the fall of 1795, the young Napoleon Bonaparte had made quite a name for himself. He had secured the command of the French army in Italy and, through a combination of bold military campaigns and masterful diplomacy, had succeeded in carving up Italy into a number of small republican states, modeled on and dependent upon France. As a reward for his success in Italy, Napoleon was given the job of heading up the offensive against England.

He approached his new task with even more than his usual daring and showmanship; he would strike at the British indirectly by invading Egypt and cutting off their access to their eastern colonial empire. The Egyptian campaign was not as successful as the Italian campaign had been and resulted in several discouraging defeats. Still, the campaign captured the imagination of the French. They were dazzled by tales of the army's adventures in this ancient and exotic land of pyramids and sphinxes, and by the triumphs of the scholars who had joined the expedition. It was during the Napoleonic campaign, for example, that the Rosetta stone, which helped Westerners decipher hieroglyphics, was discovered. In addition, Napoleon's military reports minimized his defeats and played up his victories.

When Napoleon returned to France he was hailed as a conquering hero. Along the roads to Paris the crowds of welcomers and well-wishers were at times so thick that his carriage could scarcely move. His hero's reception merely confirmed a belief Napoleon had held for some time: "[The French] need glory," he declared, "the satisfaction of their vanity; but as for liberty, they know nothing about it. . . . The nation needs a leader, a leader made illustrious by glory."

Characters in the Revolutionary Drama: *Napoleon Bonaparte*

"Nothing will ever be achieved without great men," Charles de Gaulle, former President of France, once wrote. The idea this statement expresses owes much to the legacy of Napoleon. The "great man" theory of history, which claims that history is in large measure shaped by the lives of a few great men, was formulated by nineteenth-century historians who had been awed by the impact Napoleon had on the world.

If ever a man was considered great, it was Napoleon. Many historians have traditionally referred to him as "Napoleon the Great." In one of France's well-known general histories, the volume on the early nineteenth century is titled simply "Napoleon." An entire building in Paris, the Hôtel des Invalides, has been set aside to house his remains.

What was it about Napoleon that merited such a reputation? To begin with, his military achievements alone inspire awe. At the age of twenty-seven, Napoleon masterminded a campaign that resulted in the French takeover of nearly all of Italy. By

1807 he had subdued most of continental Europe. In one of the battles that played a key role in the creation of this new French empire, the Battle of Austerlitz, Napoleon's brilliant generalship enabled him to defeat Russian and Austrian armies twice the size of the French forces.

Then there are Napoleon's masterful administrative accomplishments—the codification of the hundreds of overlapping and conflicting local legal systems into the great Napoleonic Code, the establishment of the French national educational system, and the restoration of the nation to financial stability, ending decades of financial mismanagement and mayhem.

But the legend of Napoleon's greatness rests on more than his achievements. Greatness was a part of his very being. His mind, with its astonishing memory, inexhaustible capacity for detail, razor-like clarity, and powers of concentration, awed all who knew him. From an early age he had been a voracious reader and retained an astonishing amount of what he read. Before starting any project or reaching any important decision, Napoleon insisted on gathering all the pertinent facts—and no matter how vast a store of information this might prove to be, it never seemed too much for him to digest. His mind worked so quickly, with such precision and so little wasted effort, that he was forced to rely on dictation—he could not write fast enough to keep up with his train of thought. He often unnerved others by the directness of his conversation; he wasted no words in getting to the point.

Equally astonishing was Napoleon's sheer energy and the strength and focus of will with which he directed it. "Work," he remarked late in his life, "is my element. I am born and built for work." He worked incessantly and seemingly without tiring. To avoid wasting time while traveling, he stuffed the pockets of his coach with papers, journals, and other reading in which he was behind. He regularly stayed up till four in the morning, dictating. Napoleon himself linked this superhuman capacity for work to the remarkable organization of his mind. He likened it to a chest, in which each object or business was filed in a separate drawer. "When I wish to interrupt one occupation," he said, "I shut its drawer and open another. They do not mix, and when I am busy with one I am not importuned or tired by the other."

Napoleon: For and Against

Napoleon was undeniably great—but a great *what*? For years scholars and laypersons alike have debated that question. The debate has raged for so long that at least one historian devoted an entire book to the controversy (*Napoleon: For and Against*, by Pieter Geyl).

Some have praised Napoleon as one of the founders of modern France, linking him with the revolutionaries Danton, Mirabeau, and Sieyès. Other admirers have gone even further, claiming that it was Napoleon's genius that solidified many of the dreams of the Revolution.

Napoleon is clearly in debt to the French Revolution: Without the equality of opportunity it made possible, a career as an army officer would have been out of the question for this Corsican boy. And throughout his career he remained true to the revolutionary doctrine of equality. Any man of talent, no matter what his origins, could achieve a high rank in Napoleon's regime. The Emperor Napoleon also remained faithful to the revolutionary notion of popular sovereignty. Each time he stepped up to claim a new level of power and authority—as First Consul, Consul for Life, and then Emperor—he submitted the move to the people for a vote. Thus he could always maintain that he wielded his authority by popular consent.

Also, in many respects, Napoleon can be seen as continuing the work that was begun during the Revolution. Earlier revo-

Napoleon Bonaparte is shown here at the center of the takeover of 18 Brumaire (November 9), which ended France's decade of revolution. *Versailles (Art Resource/Lauros-Giraudon).*

lutionary governments had worked to codify the nation's laws, had started to build a large national army, had begun to attempt conquest of neighboring states (in order to bring to them the Revolution). Napoleon's successful organization of the national government was, in part, following the lead of the Committee of Public Safety, which also made efforts to centralize and streamline the government.

Whether Napoleon lives or dies, whether he re-appears or not on the continent of Europe, one single motive leads me to speak of him; it is the ardent desire that the friends of liberty should entirely separate their cause from his, and that they should be careful not to confound

*the principles of the Revolution with those of the imperial govern-
ment. . . . The nations persist in considering him the defender of their
rights, at the very moment when he was their greatest enemy.*

Madame de Stael, daughter of the great financier Jacques
Necker, wrote these stinging words at the end of Napoleon's
career. She was just the first of a long line of influential men
and women who have seen Napoleon as the destroyer of the
Revolutionary vision, rather than as its child or savior. At times
likening his career to such contemporary modern dictators as
Adolf Hitler, Napoleon's detractors have been as loud in their
condemnation as his admirers have been in their praise.

They see the motivation for his actions as a sheer drive for
personal power and glory. They point out that he tossed aside
the ideal of liberty and concentrated nearly all decision making
power in his own hands, that he instituted new censorship guides
and severely curtailed the freedom of the press, that he conquered
not to spread "the ideas of 1789," but for the sake of conquest.
As Emperor, they note, Napoleon brought back an aristocracy
and a hereditary monarchy. He also re-enslaved the blacks in
the French colonies who had been set free in 1794.

"Everybody has loved me and hated me; everybody has taken
me up, dropped me, and taken me up again," Napoleon remarked
near the end of his life. One of history's greatest, to be sure—
but a great what? The debate goes on. The final verdict is not
yet in.

Sieyès and Napoleon were clearly thinking along similar lines. Not
long after his return to France, Sieyès sent Napoleon word of the plan
he was developing. At that point the plan was a secret. But by November 10 (18 Brumaire) all of France was to know. With the army
to back them, Sieyès, Napoleon, and their fellow conspirators did
away with the Directory. In its place they installed a new government

called the Consulate, headed up by three consuls. All three were to wield considerably more power than the five Directors had. One, however, who would be called "First Consul," would have authority for final decisions. The post of First Consul went to Napoleon Bonaparte.

There was to be a new constitution; plans for commissions to begin work on it were made. But, in fact, ten years after France had risen up to protest the arbitrary rule of one man, the nation had another strong man at the helm.

The Revolution Lives On

The French Revolution began as a movement for political freedom—first for the aristocracy, then for the bourgeoisie, and finally, by 1793, for all Frenchmen, down to the lowliest sans-culotte or peasant. Measured against such a yardstick, the takeover of Napoleon marks the Revolution's failure in the eyes of many. Clearly, Bonaparte's regimes—whether the Consulate or the Empire, which he founded five years later—were not those of free institutions. The Consulate had elections and legislative bodies, but these were virtually powerless. Decisions were made chiefly by the First Consul. Under the Empire, the governmental bodies were rendered still more useless.

Still, there were some permanent victories. The principles of freedom and equality before the law, which were first declared in 1789, never died. In fact, when Napoleon compiled his masterful codification of the laws of the land, the famed Napoleonic Code, guaranteees of civil rights to all citizens were permanently fixed in the French legal tradition. So, too, were the institutions of constitutional government and the authority of the people. Although the legislative bodies they created were sometimes weak, never again would the French be without constitutional government. And although voting results might occasionally be tampered with, from Napoleon's transition to Emperor down to the present, French governments would continue to seek proof of popular support by means of general referenda (votes by all citizens).

Another measure can be used for judging the success of the Revolution—that of the degree to which it transformed the hierarchical society of the old regime, for such a transformation was clearly an aim of at least the latter years of the Revolution. By this standard the society of Napoleonic France gets somewhat better marks. It was not the radically egalitarian society of which the Jacobins dreamed. Certainly the sans-culottes had failed to win the rights and economic benefits for which they had fought for so many years. Still, French society under Napoleon was very different from the rigid hierarchical society of the *ancien régime*. Many nobles had returned from exile, and a number of them had even managed to retain or retrieve their property. As Emperor, Napoleon also created a new aristocracy. But neither new nor old aristocrats any longer had the privileges and feudal incomes that had set them apart in earlier years. Their former position and power were irretrievably gone.

Only a small number of peasants had been able to benefit sufficiently from the sale of confiscated land to become self-sufficient. Still, the peasantry had been freed from its burdensome feudal dues, and some peasants had risen to the ranks of substantial landowners.

The change was most noticeable in the case of the bourgeoisie and the Church. Whereas before the Revolution Church property had accounted for over 10 percent of the country's land, by Napoleon's time the Church had been stripped of nearly all this. Napoleon did restore Catholicism to its position as the official religion of the country. However, the Church's influence in the affairs of state, and even in the daily lives of parishioners, was nothing like what it had enjoyed in former years.

It was the bourgeoisie who benefited most from the Revolution. The change in their status was of such magnitude that many historians have referred to the French Revolution as a "bourgeois revolution." The nation's merchants, financiers, lawyers, and industrialists were

By 1804 Napoleon had brought France full circle. When he crowned himself Emperor, and his wife Josephine as Empress, the nation once again had a hereditary ruler on the throne and as much royal pomp as any the nation had known under Louis XVI. *The Louvre (Art Resource/Lauros-Giraudon).*

the new ruling class. The new Constitution carefully guarded the rights of property. And just as the bourgeoisie had hoped in the decades before 1789, entry to the new aristocracy was no longer determined by birth. Instead, it was open to all on the basis of merit or achievement (often measured by the size of one's fortune).

The Revolutionary Tradition

Unlike the French Revolution, the American Revolution is generally judged a great success. Yet it was the French Revolution, not the American, that most profoundly transformed politics, thought, and culture around the world.

To begin with, it largely determined the form and direction of French politics for the entire nineteenth century. Three times—in 1830, 1848, and 1871—the French revolted against reactionary monarchs and royalists and attempted to set up a republic much as they had in 1792. Often these later revolutionaries invoked the memories of the earlier Jacobins. In all three years, Parisian streets were the sites of violence; and in 1871, when the death tolls reached twenty thousand, another Commune was declared. Just as in 1794, the first two of these later French revolutions failed and were followed by conservative reaction and a return to the rule of a powerful executive— the constitutional monarch Louis Philippe in 1830, and President Louis-Napoleon in 1848. There was even a Second Empire, inaugurated by Louis-Napoleon in 1852 in an attempt to follow in his uncle's footsteps. It was only in 1870, with the creation of the Third Republic, that the pendulum swing between revolution and reaction that had dominated French political life since 1789 came to an end and democracy was permanently established. Yet even well into the twentieth century, the memories of the initial Revolution have been a part of the consciousness of every French man and woman. During the Second World War, for example, the Free French forces boasted of having revived "the spirit of '89."

Nor did the influence of the Revolution stop at France's borders.

Throughout the last years of the eighteenth century and continuing under the rule of Napoleon, France's conquering armies exported both revolutionary ideas and revolutionary governmental structures to the states they subdued. In Holland, Belgium, Switzerland, Italy, and the German states west of the Rhine, revolts were staged against conservative rulers. In Italian and German states, new republican governments were established that, although they did not survive the departure of the French troops supporting them, helped to reshape these two nations. There were also Jacobin-inspired revolts in Ireland, Poland, and Hungary, although these ended in failure. In fact, it has been said that in the long run, the effect of the French Revolution proved more truly revolutionary abroad than it did at home.

In 1804 Ludwig Van Beethoven composed his explosive Third Symphony, the *Eroica* ("Heroic"), the longest symphony written up to that time—and dedicated to Napoleon. In the late 1790s in a rustic cottage, William Wordsworth composed his *Lyrical Ballads,* poems written in everyday language that give evidence of a spiritual presence in humble, commonplace settings. Before his death in 1851 William Turner painted landscapes and seascapes that seem a swirl of passionate energies, so far are they from a realistic depiction of clouds and waves.

In the early years of the nineteenth century, artists, writers, and musicians began to break away from the intellectual, complex, and formalized styles of earlier years. Gone were the precisely executed forms and elegant harmonies of Franz Joseph Haydn and Wolfgang Amadeus Mozart, the complex verse forms and heroic subjects of poets such as Alexander Pope and Voltaire, the drawing room scenes of the French painter François Boucher. Instead, composers, writers, and painters who have since come to be called "Romantic" began to show new depths of feeling and new, unrestrained surges of energy in their works.

As important as its effects on European political life was the profound impact the French Revolution had on culture and thought in the Western world. To a considerable degree, the great shift in the arts of Europe described above was prompted by the French Revolution. The Revolution also had a profound influence on the development of political thought. It was consideration of the events of 1789–1799, the aspirations, successes, and failures, that gave rise to an important new political theory: socialism.

Robespierre and the radical Jacobins had maintained that there could be no true freedom in the face of gross inequality. They had striven for a society in which the state would help to meet the economic needs of the working classes. Gracchus Babeuf had taken this concern a step further when he proposed that the government hold land in common and distribute crops to the citizens according to their need. In the nineteenth century such Frenchmen as Henri de Saint-Simon, Louis Blanc, and Charles Fourier continued the line of thinking Robespierre and Babeuf had begun. They proposed various schemes for transforming France into a society in which state or communal ownership and distribution of goods would help to bring about true equality. These early socialists had an eager following among the working classes, who believed that such measures were needed to truly complete the work of the Revolution.

The year 1917 witnessed the Russian Revolution. If any event in recent history has been as memorable and influential as the French Revolution, it is the Russian Revolution. And yet even that great event had its roots in the revolt of the French over a century earlier. The leader of the Russian Revolution, Vladimir Lenin, subscribed to the theories of a German socialist, Karl Marx. Marx, like the French socialists, had been deeply influenced by the Revolution of 1793, in particular by the life it gave to the idea that society can be transformed. Marx advocated a revolution that would completely transform industrial society, doing away entirely with the bourgeoisie—indeed, with all classes. The Russian Revolution is only one of the many revolutions in recent decades that took as its basis the theories of Karl Marx. The radical dreams of the first Jacobins not only have survived to the present; they have spread around the world.

It probably comes as no surprise to most people that radical and revolutionary thinkers of the last two centuries owe a debt to the men of the French Revolution. Conservative political philosophy, however, is just as indebted. The modern conservative tradition had its origins in the works of Burke and others who wrote in reaction to the French Revolution.

And all of us, whether conservative or liberal, whenever we concern ourselves with the rights of women or minorities or underdeveloped nations, are using concepts that are a direct legacy of Danton, Robespierre, Marat, and Mirabeau. There can be few legacies of more importance. It is no wonder that, for all its violence, its excesses, and its failings, the French Revolution remains one of the great events in the history of humankind.

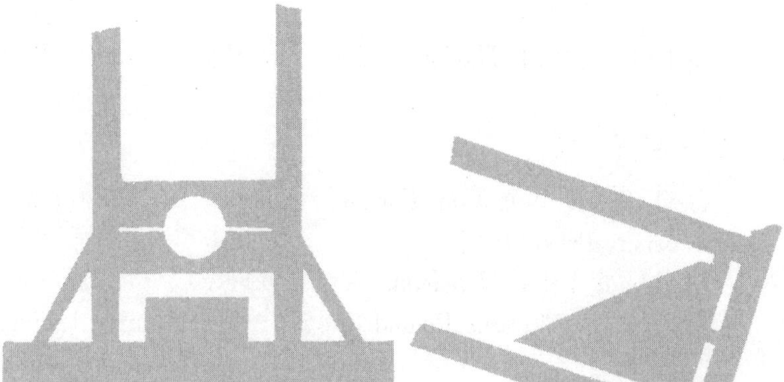

Recommended for Further Study

General Works

Furet, François, and Denis Richet. *The French Revolution*, trans. by Stephen Hardman. New York: Macmillan, 1970.

Gershoy, Leo. *The French Revolution and Napoleon*. New York: Appleton, 1964.

Hampson, Norman. *A Social History of the French Revolution*. London: Routledge, 1964.

Hibbert, Christopher. *The Days of the French Revolution*. New York: Morrow, 1980.

Sydenham, M. J. *The French Revolution*. London: B. T. Batsford, 1965.

Biographies

Geyl, Pieter. *Napoleon: For and Against*. New Haven, CT: Yale University Press, 1949.

Markham, Felix. *Napoleon*. New York: New American Library, 1963.

May, Gita. *Madame Roland*. New York: Columbia University Press, 1970.

Rudé, Georges, ed. *Robespierre, Great Lives Observed.* Englewood Cliffs, NJ: Prentice-Hall, 1967.

Thompson, J. M. *Leaders of the French Revolution.* New York: Barnes & Noble, 1968.

Wendel, Hermann. *Danton.* New Haven, CT: Yale University Press, 1935.

Specialized Subjects, Specific Viewpoints

Cobban, Alfred. *The Social Interpretation of the French Revolution.* New York: Cambridge University Press, 1964.

Doyle, William. *The Origins of the French Revolution.* New York: Oxford, 1980.

Lefebvre, Georges. *The Coming of the French Revolution,* trans. by R. R. Palmer. Princeton, NJ: Princeton University Press, 1947.

Palmer, R. R. *Twelve Who Ruled: The Committee of Public Safety During the Terror.* Princeton, NJ: Princeton University Press, 1941.

Rudé, Georges. *The Crowd in the French Revolution.* Oxford, England: Oxford, 1959.

Primary Source Material

Herold, J. C. *The Mind of Napoleon.* New York: Columbia University Press, 1955.

Higgins, E. L. *The French Revolution as Told by Contemporaries.* Boston: Houghton Mifflin, 1938.

Stewart, John Hall. *A Documentary Survey of the French Revolution.* New York: Macmillan, 1951.

Films

Children of Paradise. Marcel Carne, director; with Jean-Louis Barrault. 1946. Available for rent from Films, Inc.

Danton. Andrezj Wajda, director; with Gerard Depardieu. 1983. Available for rent from Swank.

Marie Antoinette. W. S. Van Dyke, director; with Norma Shearer and Tyrone Power. 1938. Available for rent from Films, Inc.

Napoleon. Abel Gance, director. 1926. Available for rent from Em Gee Film Library.

A Tale of Two Cities. Ralph Thomas, director; with Dirk Bogarde and Dorothy Tutin. 1958. Available for sale from Learning Corporation of America.

Fiction

Dickens, Charles. *A Tale of Two Cities.* Various publishers.

Du Maurier, Daphne. *The Glass-Blowers.* Garden City, NY: Doubleday, 1963.

Orczy, Baroness. *The Scarlet Pimpernel.* Various publishers.

Sabatini, Rafael. *Scaramouche.* Boston: Houghton Mifflin, 1921.

INDEX

References to illustrations are in *italics*.